I0462056

LEAN MADE SIMPLE
Creating Stability

David Sykes

Published by Lulu.com

First published in the UK by Lulu.com

ISBN 978-0-244-06695-6

THE AUTHOR

David Sykes is by profession a chemical engineer but has spent most of his career in manufacturing and people management and latterly as a Business and Training Consultant.

In 1988 he was first introduced to lean principles in the guise of Just in Time when his company was chosen as a JIT supplier to a major pharmaceuticals company. In 1992 he founded JIT Services, a company specialising in reducing changeover times in manufacturing companies. Since then he has applied lean principles in the various and diverse manufacturing companies he managed.

After over 35 years in manufacturing, David founded Vanilla Training Solutions in 2005, a business committed to helping organisations excel through the strategic use of the training process. He is the author of the books, Leadership, a Formula for Success and An Engineers Guide to Influencing and Persuading. He lives in Somerset with his wife Judith and their cat Flo and dog Rosie.

He can be contacted at david@theleadershipformula.uk

Acknowledgements

I would like to thank two people who have been influential in my career and an inspiration when writing this book. I would like to thank Andrew Wilson, managing director of Finidhyn® Ltd who gave me the opportunity to hone my lean skills when I worked for his company as a lean consultant on a number of ventures. If Newton said 'if I had seen further it is only by standing on the shoulders of giants', then I echo his sentiments. Andrew is truly a giant in his field; not only did he help broaden my knowledge of lean and what it could achieve, but gave me a master class in consultancy, freely sharing his knowledge through words and by example.

I would also like to thank another consultant, Adam Lenander, whose drive and enthusiasm together with a towering intellect convinced me of the wisdom of sound analysis before action. With an infectious sense of humour, our long days and evenings together passed too quickly.

I have fond memories of Andrew and Adam and our time sweating together over the detail of a project; I gained much as a consultant and as a human being. I'd like to think, by relating my experiences in management, leadership and interpersonal skills; I gave a little back, too.

I normally dedicate my books to my darling wife Judith, my soul mate and my best friend. I dedicate this book however to our children, Ian and Joanne, two of the most loving, well-balanced and caring people you could hope to meet. We are so very, very proud of them. Both devoted parents, with Tetyana and Nick they have given us six remarkable grandchildren who one day, I hope, will explore their grandfather's books.

Contents

INTRODUCTION

Have you ever been driving on a 'Smart' motorway, with the overhead signs telling you to drive at fifty miles an hour, and wondered why the slip road joining now has traffic lights? You must agree that driving on a Smart motorway at peak times is a whole lot easier than the stop-start-stop-start of an unrestricted motorway. Do you realise that you are experiencing lean in action?

How much 'management' and decision-making does it need to follow the system? None! Lane change? Why? Speed up? How? Even if the road is clear, the overhead speed cameras keep you to the calculated speed. In lean jargon, your speed is determined by the 'takt time' set by those managing the motorway. Too many cars trying to muscle in from the slip road forcing you to change lanes? Not anymore, thanks to the traffic lights. Congratulations, you are witnessing 'levelled flow' in its simplicity. Surprisingly, lean or Lean Thinking as it was called by James P Womac and Daniel T Jones of MIT when they introduced it in the nineties, is in play everywhere we look. Although it came to prominence for producing cars and has been championed by Toyota through the Toyota Production System, it is now an integral part of our daily lives.

Contrast this Smart motorway to a normal motorway where each driver tries to optimise his or her journey time. As it becomes congested, we start to make decisions. Should we change lanes now the traffic is slowing? If we do, why does our new lane suddenly go slower? What should we do next? Try cutting in, changing speed or hassle the slow driver in the wrong lane and watch our blood pressure rise as the motorway comes to a sudden halt. The reason? A lorry ahead of us has decided to overtake another on a hill! A logical decision for the lorry driver? Yes. For the productive output of the motorway? You decide!

So, who am I and what qualifies me to be your guide? My name is David Sykes and I am a chemical engineer by profession, but don't worry, I'm better now. I was first introduced to lean principles in the guise of Just in Time, in the late 1980's. I was the Manufacturing Director of a business which became a JIT supplier to a major pharmaceutical company. Amongst the many lean measures we implemented, one was replenishing their warehouse stock using Kanbans. (If you've ever picked a can of beans from a supermarket shelf, you have used a Kanban - a simple example of 'Pull' that we will discuss within the book.) My company did not own a finished goods warehouse nor did it need one. Stock, or inventory, as we will discover, is one of the seven wastes identified in lean. Finished goods from my production lines went directly to the customer, when it was wanted, where it was wanted.

In 1992 I formed a company called JIT Services, its primary purpose to reduce changeover times in manufacturing companies. Changeover time reduction or SMED as it is often called, (Single Minute Exchange of Dies) is a key element of JIT. Fast forward to 2008 and I was working as a consultant in a semiconductor factory helping the management team to implement lean manufacturing. In between, I have applied lean principals in the many manufacturing operations I have managed.

Having said this, I do not consider myself in any way an expert. If you wish to get a detailed, in-depth understanding of lean, (perhaps your company is about to carry out a full implementation), there are many good books around. My goal, in this series of books, is to simplify lean and debunk some of the mystery surrounding it. For yes, there is a lot of mystery perpetuated about lean. Some proponents, for example, insist on using the original Japanese word, 'muda', when talking about waste. Admittedly, it does sound similar to the French word 'merde' which means, well I'm sure you know what it means, but it misses the point! The point being, that whilst 'merde' is usually quite obvious, some things which most of us think of as valuable are actually quite wasteful. Read on if you wish to know what these are and why they are so wasteful.

Whilst lots of people now know of lean, the enthusiasm for adopting it is tepid in many organisations. As a consultant, one of the many arguments I have heard for not considering a lean transition, is, 'Yes, I know lean works in some businesses, but we're different!' (They then spout out one hundred good reasons why they are not the same as a car plant). Trust me, they're not different, at all! The semiconductor plant I mentioned earlier was a marvel of technology with a high proportion of PhDs managing it. The unit operations were mind-blowing in their intricacy, but the problems they faced were the same problems faced by any 'jobbing shop'. Whether its sewing machines, trouser presses and pattern cutting or photo-etch, screen oxidation and metal deposition, the problems and solutions, are the same. When, as a consultant, I went into companies to sell the idea of creating a lean operation, I always finished with the question, 'Are you brave enough?'

The kind of courage it requires, I might add, is not that faced by people in high-risk jobs. The courage required is in adopting what may appear to be radically different ways of working which at first seem counter-intuitive. It takes, at some stage, a 'leap of faith' to stop doing something which has been effective for years and change to a practice which seems, at best, to leave the operation sailing very close to the wind. In this series of books, I explain the reasons behind these counter-intuitive ideas and explains how we can minimise, if not eliminate, the risk.

There are five stages we must go through if we are to create a truly lean enterprise. This book deals with the first and most important stage, creating stability. Stability is fundamental to our lean journey, like the foundations of a house, get it wrong and the whole structure will collapse.

Who is this book written for? Primarily for those who would like to know more about lean and how it can benefit their organisation. It does not pretend to give you a comprehensive, blow-by-blow methodology required for a full lean implementation. What it will do, however, is give you an insight into the different elements of lean, in LAYMAN'S terms, which you can apply in your day to day activities, whatever enterprise you are in.

If you are a manager, supervisor or team leader considering a transition to a lean enterprise, not only do you need a broad understanding of lean, but a different approach to leadership. In the same way as driving on a Smart motorway instils in the users a different way of driving, lean systems require a different style of leadership. I call this style, Leading4Lean, a programme I developed in 2008 to assist those in leadership positions to manage within a Lean Enterprise, more effectively. I cover this in detail in the last of the books. If you wish to know more about becoming a better leader, however, I recommend that you read my book, Leadership, a Formula for Success.

So, what's in it for you? If you are at the stage of your career where you wish to broaden your understanding of lean and use some of its elements to improve the efficiency of your part of the organisation, this book is written for you. In it, I offer you real-life examples where you can see how lean principals have me helped drive up productivity in organisations as varied as packaging manufacture, bottle-blowing and a federation of three schools. If lean sounds as if it could be expensive, believe me, changes can be made at very little cost and, in the long run, are often self-financing. Whatever your reason, I guarantee that the knowledge you acquire from this book will help make your job better and easier. Trust me, I'm an engineer!

David Syl

January 2018

MODULE ONE

OVERVIEW

We might be forgiven for believing that the methods that are employed to drive efficiency in modern manufacturing operations are quite recent. Certainly, the term 'lean' has only been in vogue since the 1980's suggesting a revolution that has created new ways of 'thinning out' operations to make them more efficient.

I am sure the builders of the pyramids had their own secret ways of boosting output. Moving quickly forward, however, the first 'efficiency expert' we might recognize lived in the 17th century. His name was Isaac Newton. Already known as a brilliant scientist, in 1699 he was invited to become 'Master of the Royal Mint'. The reason? 'Crimpers' or criminals who 'snipped' off the edges of coins to make counterfeit coins, were devaluing and debasing the currency, forcing the Royal Mint to remake all the coinage which was in circulation. This was a massive task and, with the methods of production available to them at the time, the Mint was unable to keep pace with the crimpers. Enter Isaac Newton who applied his genius to reorganise the production process and, using a production line of 500 men, replaced England's complete money supply in just four years. Hardly lean, but an early example of using brain power as well as manpower for 'mass-production'.

Mass production of cars using an assembly line was first introduced by Henry Ford in 1913 and his techniques were used during World War II to mass produce bombers, tanks, and even ships. It was in the 1950's, however, when Toyota in Japan began to refine and rethink these techniques and introduced what is known as TPS. - The Toyota Production System. Perhaps the more revolutionary element of TPS occurred in the 1960's when Toyota brought their suppliers into the programme, training them to use the same techniques, one of which was Just in Time. (JIT)

In 1975, JIT began to spread across other Japanese companies. Another technique, Kaizen also became commonplace and if you are not familiar with the term, it relates to the Japanese philosophy of continually improving working practices, personal efficiency etc. We will discuss it later in the programme under the more generic term, Continuous Improvement (CI).

By 1980, the Western world began to take notice of Japanese manufacturing techniques and a number of books on the subject became popular further spreading the word. Amongst them is Japanese Manufacturing Techniques published in 1982 by Richard J Schonberger who then went on to write World Class Manufacturing in 1986. Adding to the debate was an Israeli scientist called Eliyahu M Goldratt who in 1984 wrote The Goal, a novel which introduced a new philosophy for businesses known as OPT, Optimised Processing Technology. All are still of value today and certainly worth reading.

By the mid-eighties, the USA, Canada, and Europe were starting to employ these Japanese manufacturing techniques in the automotive sector and in companies such as Hewitt Packard and Black and Decker.

In 1990, the term lean was introduced in the book, The Machine that Changed the World by James P Womac and Daniel T Jones from MIT. It contrasted the old methods of manufacturing, mass production with the different business system employed by Toyota which they identified as lean. They demonstrated that, by having a completely different business philosophy, Toyota overtook Ford and GM to become the largest and most successful enterprise in the world. In 1996, they continued to develop their ideas with their book, Lean Thinking.

In this book, the elements of Japanese manufacturing techniques of the 1950's and 1960's were combined with others, particularly value stream mapping, to introduce a distinct methodology we now know as Lean Thinking. We will discuss all these concepts as we progress through the book.

So, what exactly is lean? There are many 'definitions, for example:

- A collection of tools and techniques commonly used by world-class manufacturing companies
- An inspirational philosophy and vision
- A practical methodology to help guide operational improvements

Or, to use the words of Womac and Jones:

"lean thinking is lean because it provides a way to do more and more with less and less...

...while coming closer and closer to providing customers with exactly what they want"

We can all relate to the idea of doing more with less, this is the fundamental basis of increasing both efficiency and productivity in any operation. (We will define these words later).

The dilemma for manufacturers is that the traditional ways of improving efficiencies, such as increasing batch sizes or reducing the range of products offered to those that are easily manufactured, are in direct conflict to the second part of the definition, 'coming closer and closer to what the customers want'.

So, quite a challenge there! In theory, if the customer wants one item, we must move towards manufacturing one item. If the customer now wants bells and whistles, well, start ordering the bells!

Mass production became efficient by reducing variety and complexity through restricting the customer's choice. Originally, Henry Ford said that the customer could have any colour they wanted, as long as it was black! Lean addresses the challenge of how customers can have any colour, in a quantity approaching one, without compromising the efficiency advantages that a volume production line offers. It is clear, therefore, that if we are to convince people of the benefits of lean, we need to change people's mindsets. In fact,

The principle barrier to implementing lean successfully involves changing people's mindsets and behaviours

So what benefits might we expect from lean?   Typically, companies who implement lean can expect to see:
- Productivity increases by 50 - 100%
- Production lead times reduce by 90%
- Inventories reduce by 90%
- Space requirement reduces by 50%
- A dramatic improvement in bottom line profits and customer service.
- Employees feeling more empowered as people are engaged at every level

Clearly prizes worth striving for!   Let us continue our overview by looking at these barriers and contrast the traditional methods employed by companies with those employed by world-class manufacturers, such as Toyota.

Quality

I recall seeing a cartoon in the early eighties where two old-school industrialists are puffing their cigars as they watched their old factory building being demolished. "I fear, Caruthers," said one industrialist to the other, "the good old days of cheap and nasty have gone!"

And for some, (not the customers, obviously!) they were the good old days. Quality was inspected into a product in the hope that the inspectors would capture all the defects. Businesses worked to AQL levels (Acceptable Quality levels) where depending on the level agreed with the customer, they were allowed so many defects per 10,000. There is a story of a Japanese company who completed their first delivery to a UK customer. The Quality Department had specified an 'acceptable' defect level of 10 rejects per 10,000 products. The main delivery came to the warehouse with a little package accompanying it. When it was opened by the Quality Manager there were 10 units inside with a little note attached. 'We have enclosed the ten rejects as per your instructions' it read. 'We have packed these separately so as not to contaminate your stock.'

In the car industry and many others, there was a phenomenon known as the 'Friday afternoon special'. The workers, no doubt de-mob happy at the thought of the weekend, were slip-shod in their work. Some poor, unsuspecting customer would pay the bill for this transgression for the next ten years.

Contrasting this, with world-class operations, Statistical Process Control (SPC) is in use to monitor the process and thereby avoid the conditions that produce defects. Defects per 10,000 is no longer a measure; defects, if any, are measured in parts per million. (ppm). Manufacturing operations are simplified and the cause of irregularities engineered out.

Production

Before lean and Japanese manufacturing techniques took hold, the answer to getting output from a business was to 'push' work through the factory. In non-lean companies, production is scheduled in batches and the concept of an economic batch quantity is used to ensure profitability. Sub-assemblies are commonplace and stored in Work In Progress (WIP) buffers to ensure material is always to hand. These sub-assemblies are then incorporated into the main product in a series of assembly operations.

19

In world-class manufacturing operations, products are assembled in-line where all the components are brought together in a continuous process. This is also known as 'one-piece flow'. Instead of pushing work through the factory, it is pulled through, the demand being created at the despatch department, not the planning department. Material Resource Planning (MRP II) might play a part in tracking material requirements and usage, but is no longer the engine of the business.

Where assembly work is required, this is done in a production cell where flow between workstations is optimised and WIP is kept to a minimum.

Maintenance

In old-style companies, machines are run until they break down. This reactive style of maintenance, waiting for parts to fail, creates instability and uncertainty.

World-class companies are proactive in their approach to maintenance, employing TPM – Total Preventative Maintenance. Instead of equipment breaking down at the most inopportune time, they are taken out of service periodically to be maintained.

Employees

Traditional companies still employ a form of demarcation, where workers have specialist skills and are called on to use them, for example for line changeovers which are done primarily by the engineering department. Piecework may still be used as an incentive to increase production.

In a modern, world-class company, workers are multi-skilled. Instead of calling the specialist, the workers have the necessary skills within their team to handle most eventualities. Assembly work is organised into self-contained cells containing all the resources and skills required to complete the task.

Systems

In traditional manufacturing companies, Command and Control systems are in place to assist the push of material through the plant. Computerised Material Requirement Planning systems (MRP) were initially installed to ensure materials were to hand and this has evolved into MRP II to incorporate the other resources needed.

World class companies, on the other hand, practice Kaizen or continuous improvement where workgroups can introduce their own systems relevant to the task. Instead of a vast, plant-wide system, many small, bespoke systems are in place.

It may be, in your own organisation, you recognise elements of the old and the new. We will explain some of the terms introduced as we progress through the book, but first, let us look at one of the key planks of lean, the control of waste.

VALUE AND WASTE

What are our ultimate goals if we are to implement lean? Are you sitting down?

Zero defects. Zero downtime. Zero inventory. Zero delay. Zero paperwork.

Quite a challenge, I can hear you thinking. Lean, however, is a journey rather than a destination. Surely it is better to aim for perfection and miss than to settle for mediocrity? Let us start our lean journey, therefore, by understanding the importance of the two key principles in Lean Thinking - Value and Waste.

By VALUE we are referring to the value a customer finds in our product or service. As such it is not concrete, such as weight or colour, but subjective. For example, we all have remote controllers for our TVs and DVD/Blu-Ray players. How many of the buttons on these ever more complex remote controllers do we value? Without a doubt, the sound adjustment and channel change buttons are indispensable, but what about the others? Their value will depend on our level of interest and understanding of the sophistication of the product. Value may be defined better by considering the alternative, Waste. So what do we mean by waste? In lean terms:

WASTE is anything other than the minimum amount of equipment, materials, parts, space and employee's time which are **absolutely essential** to add value to the product or service.

The two key words here are, 'absolutely essential'. To explain this definition further, Jones and Womac asked us to think in terms of the (customer) value we create. Digressing slightly, in 'the Goal' which I mentioned earlier, Goldratt defined the purpose of a business, the 'goal,' is to make money. Anything that does not make us money, therefore, is superfluous. In the same way, any activity we undertake which does not add VALUE to the product, (please note, unlike Goldratt, value is not always monetary) is probably waste.

To test whether an activity is waste, we can ask three questions:

- Does the event or action physically transform the product in some way? If so it probably adds value.
- If the customer observed the event, would he or she recoil from the cost? If so, the event probably does not add value.
- If the event were eliminated, would the customer know the difference? If not, the event is probably non-value added.

I think we all can agree that turning a piece of silicon into a microchip adds value. Turning the microchip into a computer or tablet clearly adds further value. Point 1 is therefore satisfied for the customers of the tablet or computer.

What about the next test? We are all familiar with the iPad. Prior to the iPad, the computer market in the early noughties was moving towards netbooks. These were small laptops with a screen, a keyboard and a mouse and many different type of ports to interface with printers, the mouse, keyboard, etc. Nothing superfluous there, then, or is there? 'I beg to differ,' said Steve Jobs, the co-founder of Apple.

To prove it, he introduced the iPad. It had a screen, yes, the essential part of any computer. But it did not have a mouse, a keyboard, or any interface ports. The iPad is the ultimate lean computer experience; Steve Jobs considered himself a minimalist. His message to the world; 'Simplicity is the Ultimate Sophistication.'

It was not all plain sailing. Some of his colleagues wanted a stylus to use with the on-screen keyboard. Jobs resisted. 'We already have 10 styluses', he argued, 'the digits on our hands. Why do we need another?' Would a stylus have added value to the iPad? Would the customers, happy to use their fingers, have resisted the additional cost? Most likely. A stylus, therefore, would not have added value. Point 2 is therefore satisfied.

Of course, it was never offered. Did the customer know the difference? No, point 3 is satisfied.

In the process of developing the iPad, although he was not a known champion of lean, Jobs used, by our definition, 'the minimum amount of equipment, materials, parts, space and employee's time which were **absolutely essential** to add value to the product or service.'

Lean, please note, does not mean doing everything on the cheap. The iPad is still an expensive piece of kit but delivers its purpose in a very lean way.

THE 7 WASTES

Waste to most people has connotations of scrap or defects. Lean Thinking defines waste in seven distinct areas, applicable to all enterprises and not just manufacturing. These are Overproduction, Waiting, Transportation, Over-processing, Inventory, Scrap/Rework and Motion.

I can image when first looking at the list, the thought occurs, 'how can be transportation be considered waste or even inventory which we need to run our operation?' To explain, let us start with overproduction.

Overproduction

Overproduction occurs when the product is manufactured in excess of customer demand or in advance of customer demand. To rephrase this it means making too much of something or making it before it is needed. Why is it a waste? By overproducing we use resources unnecessarily; these include people, material, and machinery. It creates unnecessary inventory and contributes to other forms of waste. For example, if a machine is continually in use, it cannot be maintained which could lead to a break down later.

Let us consider an office and how overproduction can become actual waste. Have you ever printed off forms you use regularly, for example, a holiday request form? Perhaps you decided to produce extra only to find out someone has later changed the format and the ones you have stored are no longer accepted? The forms sit idly gathering dust or they end up being used for scrap paper. Sounds familiar? The lesson, whether in the office or the factory, is only we should only produce what we immediately need.

In the 1990's, I started a company called JIT Services, the main purpose of which was to help manufacturing companies reduce changeover times. In our later discussions on productivity, we will see that when a machine is not producing it is not recovering overheads and what are known as 'standard labour hours'. The quicker the machine is changed over, therefore, the smaller the loss of productive time.

I wrote the chairman of one of leading manufacturing companies in the area where I lived and was invited to see the managing director. He asked me to investigate a printing machine which was running flat out, 24 hours a day, seven days a week. The production director had raised a request to buy a second machine but at a million pounds sterling it was a big investment. Before spending this considerable amount of money, the MD wanted to be sure the current machine was fully utilised.

Once on the factory floor, I asked questions of the shift manager. Although changeover times were clearly a factor, it became clear that there was more involved in the machine being over utilised. Because there were so many changeovers, the shift manager was running every order an extra 10% above the amount stated on the works order; the customer specification actually allowed him to do this. To him, it seemed a logical step to ease the situation but his extra 10% was in fact waste in the form of overproduction. Why did it matter? Well, changeovers took 50% of the available time, so for the other 50%, he was overproducing by 10%. A considerable portion of his available production time, therefore, was used in producing goods that were not required. Although it was 'good stock', it was still 'waste' and a major contributing factor to the problem.

By stopping overproduction and other lean measures particularly streamlining the changeover process, after two days output was so high that they produced in 10 shifts what it had taken 21 shifts to produce! Needless to say, the production director did not get his new machine.

Transportation

The transportation of material or parts may at first appear necessary to most organisations but on further examination, it adds no value to the process. Instead of value, transport requires extra resources in terms of people, material, and equipment. Transportation also needs some form of management and temporary storage locations. Additionally, the more a part is handled the more likely it is to be damaged. Transportation of material leads to increased inventory and potential delays elsewhere in the manufacturing process. In the office, our over-produced forms have to be transported to their temporary store and then a 'management' decision made as to what to do with them.

In the example of the overworked printing machine, when the changeover commenced, the operator first had to go to the parts store and bring the changeover parts to the line. The solution was to locate the parts at the side of the printing machine thereby eliminating their transportation during the changeover.

Waiting

Waiting occurs in a manufacturing operation when either material or operators wait for machines to complete cycles of work. Waiting in an office environment might include the time you stand at the photocopier waiting for the unnecessary forms to print off.

Although modern machines generally do not require watching them whilst in automatic operation, often an operator cannot start the machine because he or she is waiting for materials or personnel or instructions. Waiting causes a delay in the processing time and, in almost every type of operation, is one area where we can make big gains to improve output and hence productivity.

Inventory

Inventory is any quantity of parts or material held within the system which is not being worked on. Most businesses rely on inventory to avoid delays and waiting time. It covers for unresponsive and unreliable processes; however, it takes up floor space, requires management and ties up cash. It is only of value when it is used. When considering moving to JIT, inventory is the buffer that hides all the problems that need to be resolved before JIT can be fully implemented.

Another downside of inventory is that it can become obsolete or spoil or if in a warehouse, damaged or contaminated. It never ceases to amaze me how much obsolete stock businesses carry, usually because of overproduction and poor stock control. The car industry has made massive inroads into reducing inventory by operating lean manufacturing. If you think of all the thousands of components that go into making a car, if you had to store only one day's inventory, you would need a massive warehouse. The car makers overcome the need for storing components by having their suppliers operate 'Just in Time'. Components ranging from car seats to carpets and steering wheels are delivered directly to the side of the production line as and when they are needed. Often the delivery wagon will collect the parts required from a number of different suppliers such that they are delivered to the workstation together.

Inventory, despite its appearance as an asset on the balance sheet, is considered by some lean exponents to be 'evil'. It devours the capital that a business needs to grow, devours valuable floor space and increases material handling.

Inventory does have its advantages, however, and as such, is not in itself a problem. It is actually an effect. Like fat is a symptom of a poor diet and lack of exercise, inventory is often a symptom of poor factory layout, poor scheduling, and insufficient maintenance.

Over-processing

Over-processing is where resource or effort is applied to a product or process that adds cost but no value for the customer. Quite often we add 'bells and whistles' to something which the end user does not require and certainly would not pay for if they were asked. This is the waste most people have difficulty relating to. We have already seen that by adding a stylus to the iPad, it would not have added value. A simple example in the office environment might be unnecessary signatures on an approval process or even, re-reading emails again and again instead of dealing with them when they arrive. In manufacturing, the solution is to specify the customer requirements exactly and ensure they are not exceeded.

Scrap/Rework

Any manufactured product which does not meet customer requirements after the normal process is clearly a waste. Poor process discipline, inadequate training, poor design of facilities and equipment, poor levels of process stability and capability, careless handling of material, can all contribute to this form of waste.

Rework is often viewed as a lesser "evil" but the time spent whilst reworking defective parts means the loss of further good parts from the process. If we consider the labour hours recovered, reworking a product does not recover any hours as these were already accounted for on first making the product. Whilst defects are a fact of life, they are not inevitable and every effort should be made in processes and procedures to minimise the production of defects.

Motion

Any motion by operators or machines when carrying out cycles of work which does not add value is also waste. Even the best processes require some motion by operators or machines which does not strictly add value. This type of waste is referred to as 'incidental motion'. Incidental motion is that which is necessary within the current process design, such as taking parts from a pallet, loading and unloading a machine, starting the machine etc.

Any other motion, such as walking, reaching, lifting and lowering is total waste. A classic example of motion as a waste occurs in the office where the printer is separate from the workstation. Once the printing is completed, the office worker then has to walk to the printer to collect their work. Shared printers might appear a good way of saving money but when one examines it in terms of 'lean' they contribute to waste by unnecessary motion and waiting.

All motion must be minimised. Re-laying the work area to reduce motion by placing processes next to each other can have a significant impact and is often easy to achieve.

Whilst elimination of waste is a key element of lean, and can, of course, be used in non-lean enterprises, we need to consider the other items in our lean 'toolkit' before we can progress to a lean enterprise.

Before we begin this journey, let us start with a basic understanding of the needs of a business and how businesses develop.

MODULE 2

HOW A BUSINESS DEVELOPS

It is useful to take a pause at this stage of our lean journey, and consider how businesses form and then develop. This will give us an insight into the when the time is right to introduce lean.

THE NEEDS OF A BUSINESS

Psychologists tell us that humans have needs. An industrial psychologist called Abraham Maslow proposed these are organised into a hierarchy, where the lowest needs have to be satisfied first before we can consider the next need. This is also true of a business. The lowest need of a business is DEMAND. Whatever our product, be it widgets or aeroplanes, there has to be a demand for it before anything can happen. I remember reading a book on business where it made the observation, 'nothing happens until somebody sells something'. Without a product to sell and someone to promote it, then a business cannot progress.

The salesperson required to promote it is, therefore, a RESOURCE, which together with capital investment, people and equipment and know-how, are needed to satisfy the demand. This is the second need of a business.

The resources in themselves do not necessarily satisfy the Demand, we need a PLAN or strategy to dictate how the resources must be used to meet the demand. This is the third need of a business.

If we are successful, we will be effective as the Resources satisfy the Demand. EFFECTIVENESS is the fourth need of a business. Surprisingly is not always achieved, I might add. Many businesses struggle to meet customer demand effectively and sometimes end up throwing more resources at the problem, usually people. Unless the extra people are fully trained, which may not always be the case; they can add further problems in trying to meet the demand.

If we are successful in being Effective the ultimate need of a business is EFFICIENCY. To become efficient, it involves reducing the amount of resources and changing the plan to continue to be effective; not an easy task. Perversely, although efficiency is the highest order of a business, some companies drive for efficiency before they are even effective, with disastrous results.

I have illustrated the hierarchal needs of a business below:

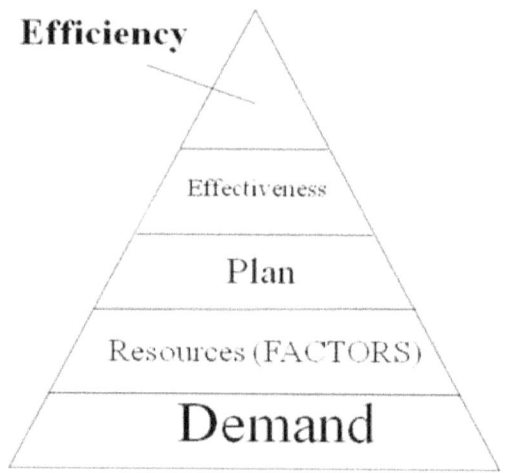

Clearly, this book is focussed on implementing a lean strategy to ensure that the minimum amount of resources is used to meet the demand. In the process of achieving this, we will become effective and then efficient. We will discuss these two terms in detail, later in the book, when we discuss metrics and productivity.

BUSINESS DEVELOPMENT

Having an understanding of the five needs of a business, let us look again at business development and the five stages the people involved in it must go through to become effective and then efficient. These are:

Innocence – Awareness – Understanding – Competence – Excellence

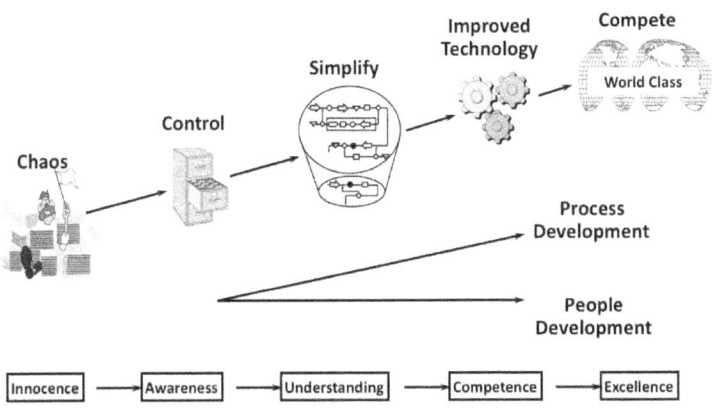

In the first stage, **innocence**, we also have chaos. The degree may differ, but the drive to fulfil demand and acquire the resources needed is initially quite chaotic. The second law of thermodynamics tells us that chaos is the natural order of the universe. I have been in enough failing businesses to agree with this prognosis!

Fortunately, as the people responsible for the business begin to tackle the lack of order, they start to take control. This **awareness** leads to Command and Control systems appearing together with measures, called metrics to identify the difference between the 'what is' to the 'what should be.'

The control and command systems create **understanding** and this is when a business that seeks to become world-class, begins to look at reducing complexity in their operation. If they choose the lean path, then simplification becomes the order of the day.

Competence, through better ways of working and the introduction of new technologies, ultimately leads to **excellence** and a world-class operation. The key stage in this development is awareness and this is when we need to have the correct metrics in place. We are getting ahead of ourselves, however, let us return to the subject of lean and consider the elements or individual pieces that make up the lean 'jigsaw'. In our model of business needs, lean thinking forms part of the 'plan' and is introduced during the 'understanding' phase.

THE LEAN JIGSAW

We have already mentioned Just In Time, but let us look at, briefly, the other pieces of the lean jigsaw before we see how they fit into place.

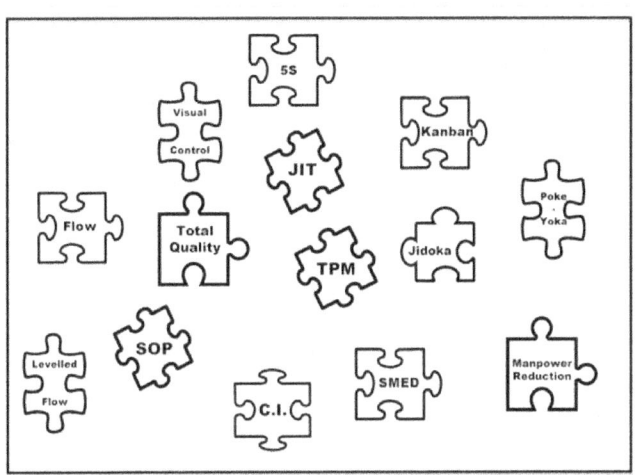

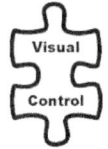 **JIT** – a system that recognises exactly what the customer wants and tries to satisfy that requirement exactly. Its main focus is on Lead-Time Reduction and hence increased flexibility. Ideally, the exact amount of parts required arrive the moment they are needed at the place where they are consumed.

Visual Control – a technique used in businesses where information is communicated directly using visual signals rather than text or other written instructions allowing quick recognition.

 **Kanban** – originally the Japanese word for signboard. A Kanban system is a means of visual

35

control that links customer demands directly to production. It is a simple system of replenishment; the "kanbans" signal production as to what is needed, when it is needed and the amount needed. It can be a card, as used in the supermarkets for high-value goods, or an empty square on the floor.

 **Total Quality** – instead of inspection and rejection, TQM or Total Quality Management is a management approach which involves everyone in the organization being involved in the quality process.

Continuous Improvement – Also known as Kaizen, is the ongoing effort to improve all aspects of the process and products, not with a 'breakthrough' improvement, but with steady, incremental steps.

Jidoka – this is one of the two pillars of TPS, the other being JIT. Jidoka highlights the problems by stopping work immediately. The root cause of the problem can then be identified and the defect rectified through the continuous improvement process.

Flow Manufacturing – unlike batch production, flow manufacturing is production using a continuous process that takes in raw materials and converts these to a finished product in a series of in-line operations.

Levelled Production – is when the rate of production remains constant irrespective of the fluctuation in demand. Its purpose is to maximise plant capacity utilisation whilst maintaining the workforce level. Levelled production is a key element of TPS.

 **Standard Operations** - A Standard Operation is centred around human movements, outlining efficient, safe working methods that eliminate waste whilst ensuring proper use of equipment and tooling.

TPM – Total Preventative Maintenance, as we introduced earlier, is a system of maintaining and improving the integrity of equipment by involving the users as well as specialists

 **SMED** – originally standing for Single Minute Exchange of Dies, it is an approach to the rapid changeover of a manufacturing process from one product to another.

 **Poke-Yoka** – a mechanism that helps an operator avoid mistakes and prevents defects.

Manpower reduction – one of the outcomes of employing lean techniques. Although not the sole purpose of a lean implementation, it often follows.

5S – A workplace organisation method that follows the logic of 'a place for everything and everything in its place'. A fundamental step in creating the stability required for a lean operation.

If this is your first introduction to some of these terms, don't worry, we will be considering a wider definition as we progress. It is useful to remind ourselves of the words of Daniel T Jones:

"the tools don't work in isolation - a deeper logic connects them" - *the logic of process and people – Professor Daniel T Jones*

STARTING OUR JOURNEY

With the jigsaw pieces now in front of us, how do we put them together to complete the picture? In fact, what is the picture? I said earlier, the elements of lean can be used separately, and on closer examination, many of them have been in play for a very long time. If we truly wish to benefit from lean, however, we must have our sights set on the ultimate prize: World Class Manufacturing.

So, what is WCM? Here's the rub, there is not a standard definition we can work to! In his book, World Class Manufacturing, Richard Schonberger uses the Latin words for, 'faster, higher, stronger.' A modern translation might be continual and rapid improvement.

Some definitions of WCM consider the processes that are in place whilst others define it in terms of performance. All agree, however, that WCM organisations deliver exceptional performance that is recognised as a benchmark by its industry sector.

There is general agreement that WCM involves four distinct principles:

JIT , TQM, TPM and Employee Involvement (EI)

A recent addition to the quest for World Class is known as Opex or Operational Excellence. This combines all the elements of WCM together with benchmarking with other, similar organisations.

Let us use these four distinct principles, JIT, TQM, TPM and EI as the basis for beginning to assemble our jigsaw.

THE FIVE-STEP PROCESS

There are five key steps we must go through if we are to become World Class. These are:

1. Achieve Process Stability
2. Establish Continuous Flow
3. Introduce Pull
4. Introduce Level Scheduling
5. Refine operations through Continuous Improvement

The first step, as you might expect, is the most critical. It is the bedrock on which we are to build our world-class operation.

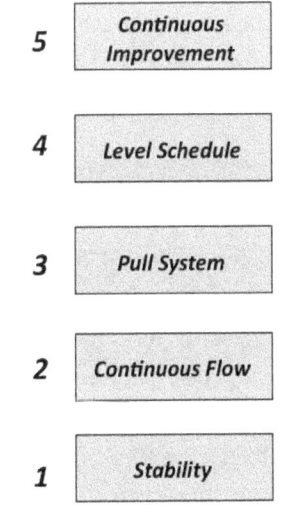

At this stage the combined effects of reduced inventory, better visual controls and workforce involvement can lead to a virtous improvement spiral.

Once the cells are beginning to perform, inventory can be taken out of the system and shop floor production controls take over from complex IT systems.

Often, improving flow requires a change in plant layout and installing cellular manufacturing. These changes require a committed workforce, top level support and careful planning.

In my experience, lean manufacturing can not be successfully exploited without having first installed management control systems and addressed quality issues.

THE FIVE-STEP PROCESS

STEP ONE - PROCESS STABILITY

The first and most important step if we are to succeed in implementing lean and becoming world-class is to achieve process stability. Creating stability is the focus of this book. To do this there are five key areas we must address;.

1 Management Control and Reporting Systems (MCRS)
2 Problem-solving teams
3 Standard operations
4 Equipment reliability
5 Workshop organisation

We will review the other four steps together with the management style needed in a lean operation in Books 2 and 3.

Recalling our discussions of the development of a business, we see it moving from innocence to awareness to understanding. The key to awareness and understanding is to have the correct Management Control and Reporting system (MCRS) in place. Unless our current business is at the innocent/chaotic state, we will already have a set of Key Performance Indicators (KPIs) by which we measure performance. Let us now consider the subject of measures or metrics and KPIs.

MANAGEMENT CONTROL AND REPORTING SYSTEMS

Metrics and Key Performance Indicators

If we are to become world-class, we need to introduce, not only the right lean tools and techniques but also a series of measures to know how well we are progressing in achieving our goals. Without a way of measuring our progress, we have no way of knowing if we are succeeding. There is a classic tale about the passengers relaxing on an aeroplane after a somewhat bumpy takeoff. As usual, the captain came on the intercom to speak to the passengers, but it was not what they were expecting. "Ladies and gentlemen", he said, "I would just like you to know that our instruments have gone down. We have no idea where we are and have no idea where we are heading. I want to assure you, however, that we are going as fast as we can!"

Going fast in the wrong direction only compounds the problem. Let us consider, therefore, the metrics, or measures that we can use to help us on our journey.

METRICS

When we use the term metric, we are referring to a direct numerical measure that represents a piece of data that is of value to us if we are to achieve our goal. An example in a business selling to other businesses or to the general public might be: "gross sales by week." In this case, the measure would be pounds (gross sales) and the dimension would be time (week). For a given measure, we may also want to see the values across different hierarchies, for example, by day, by week or by month.

For most enterprises, we need to have a balanced set of metrics. For example, if the organisation we are considering is a manufacturing organisation, we would expect to see metrics reporting output and waste. We would also expect to see measures of financial performance. There is a way of balancing out the metrics applicable to any enterprise, to ensure it focuses on the most important areas. It is commonly called the Balanced Scorecard.

The concept was developed in the early 90s by two guys from Harvard Business School; Robert Kaplan and David Nor-ton. At the time, most companies predominantly used financial measures to control their business. Though clearly necessary they can only report what has happened in the past. It is like driving your car by looking in the rear-view mirror!

Without going into too much detail, Kaplan and Norton proposed that enterprises should look at a range of metrics covering the key areas of fundamental to success. The Balanced Scorecard they proposed was, in fact, a management system although it does include measurements.

They considered that the four areas a business should focus on were:

- Customer Metrics – this is the measure of customer satisfaction

- Financial Metrics – tracking financial requirements and performance
- Internal Business Processes – The things they must be good at to succeed
- Learning and Growth – Improving and creating value

The metrics for these four key areas are usually aligned with the Vision and Mission and the Strategy of the organisation. Since then, businesses have adapted this concept and often a people dimension is included. Measures for these key areas can then be decided and included in the reporting systems. I am sure you will be already familiar with your own organisation's reporting systems and the associated KPIs; these tend to be the triggers for beating managers over the head at regular frequencies!

KEY PERFORMANCE INDICATORS (Kpis)

A KPI is simply a metric that is tied to a target. Most often a KPI represents how far a metric is above or below a pre-determined target. KPIs usually are shown as a ratio of actual to target and are designed to instantly let a business user know if they are on or off their plan without the end user having to consciously focus on the metrics being represented.

Percent On-time

WIP

Defects/Yields

Costs Per Unit Output

Labour Hours

For instance, we might decide that in order to hit our quarterly production target we need to be making 10,000 widgets per week. The metric would be widget produced per week; the target would be 10,000.

If we used a gauge as the means of visualising this KPI and we had made 8,000 widgets by Wednesday, the user would instantly see that they were at 80% of their goal. When selecting targets for our KPIs we need to remember that a target will have to exist for every item we want to view within a metric.

Having a dashboard that displays a KPI for gross production by day, week, and month will require that we have set targets for each of the metrics we have identified. It is highly likely that your organisation already has metrics in place and your first thought might be, 'what's this got to do with me?'

Quite often the metrics put in place are the wrong metrics and drive the wrong behaviours within the organisation. There is a classic story of a plague of flies in China. To reduce the massive infestation the communist government offered a bounty for every dead fly. The idea being that it would incentivise the citizens to kill all the flies. Can you image what happened instead? Of course, citizens began killing flies in earnest in order to get their rewards. When the fly population dropped dramatically, people started breeding flies and then killing them! The wrong metrics and the wrong KPIs will drive the wrong behaviours!

I worked for a time as a consultant in a semiconductor manufacturing operation, commonly known as a Fab. One KPI the managers were measured by and were also incentivised in the bonus scheme was the number of wafers started into the Fab (called 'Ins') per month. They also had a bonus target for the number of Outs. Outs, as the name suggests are the wafers leaving the Fab each month. Getting production through the facility was a torturous effort because of all the highly specialised processing required, one of the reasons my colleagues and I were engaged as consultants. Starting wafers, however, was easy; literally, you just put them 'through the wall'. Which would you focus on if you want your bonus? Needless to say, 'outs' were always well below target every month as the Fab became congested with unprocessed wafers. The 'starts' target was always met! This particular metric was driving the wrong

43

behaviours and was a major contributing factor in the congestion. It was as counter-productive as the bonus for the dead flies!

Just because the company has a definite set of measures to report does not mean we have to drive output by the same measures. In the semiconductor example above, we persuaded the management to put in place a different set of KPIs which were designed to drive the right behaviours. The KPIs worked and the starts and outs fell into place accordingly. Head Office in the USA was never aware of the new KPIs. The lesson they learned was FIND THE RIGHT METRICS TO DRIVE THE RIGHT BEHAVIOURS.

SCORECARDS, DASHBOARDS, AND REPORTS

The difference between a scorecard, dashboard, and a report can be one of fine distinction. Each of these tools can combine elements of the other, but at a high level, they all target distinct and separate levels of the business decision-making process.

Scorecards

Starting at the highest, most strategic level of the business decision-making spectrum, we have scorecards. Scorecards are primarily used to help align operational execution with business strategy.

Dashboards

We mentioned earlier the need to add KPIs to a Dashboard. Think of it as the dashboard in your car. A dashboard falls one level down in the business decision-making process from a scorecard; it is less focussed on a strategic objective and more tied to specific operational goals.

In the training sessions, I ask delegates to choose three instruments from their own car dashboard which are essential to drive by. Most cars now look like aeroplane cockpits with gauges and dials, switches and warning lights. After some debate, the ones often chosen are these, with the reasons given:

- Speedometer – so we know how fast we are going and do not break the law
- Fuel Gauge – so we know how much petrol we have at any time
- The Oil Warning Light – so we don't run the engine dry

We could also choose the engine temperature gauge in case we overheat the engine, but since most cars have a sealed cooling system the risk is much less than running out of oil which is in our control.

Reports

Probably the most prevalent tool seen in business today is the traditional report. Reports can be very simple and static in nature, such as a list of sales transactions for a given time period, to more sophisticated cross-tab reports.

Summarising the Module so far, we know what we are trying to achieve as a team and have an understanding of the measures or KPIs we need to put into place to track our progress. Somewhere within those goals and measures will be activities which are geared to improving the efficiency and productivity of the business or organisation. What do I mean by efficiency?

One of the metrics included in our Management Control and Reporting System is efficiency. We have already introduced the idea of effectiveness, but what about efficiency which we know is the highest need of any organisation. Let us look at some definitions.

EFFICIENCY AND EFFECTIVENESS

To define efficiency we have to look at the basis of any production process, whether cars or children with life skills. Production is the process of converting INPUTS to OUTPUTS. Output is usually measured over a period of time so it could be cars per hour or children meeting the standard per school year. Typically reported output of a business might be the quantity of the product produced and the profit generated, both over a set period of time. A process is considered to be EFFICIENT when:

"A given quantity of OUTPUTS cannot be produced with any less INPUTS"

The "Rate of EFFICIENCY is simple the amount of (or value of) OUTPUTS divided by the amount of (or value of) INPUTS.

To explain the difference between Effectiveness and Efficiency let us consider an organisation called the Widget Company making and selling widgets. The demand for widgets is 10,000 per week or 2,000 per day. The widget manufacturing process employs 5 people and working together they produce 400 widgets each per day.

The business gets a new MD who decides to drive for efficiencies so he tells the works manager to reassess the process and cut the workforce. The works manager protests but to no avail. He buys a piece of kit to automate part of the line and reduces the workforce (Resource) to four persons. With the new kit, each employee is now producing 450 widgets per day, a 12.5% increase in efficiency! The MD is happy, his efficiencies are improving. Unfortunately, the customers are not! Output is now down to 9,000 widgets per week (450 x 4 x 5) and the Demand is still 10,000. The sales team have to start to ration deliveries. In the drive for Efficiency, the MD has made the business no longer Effective. Clearly, a new Plan, as with our business hierarchy, is required to bring it back into balance. The key learning for the Widget Company is 'Become EFFECTIVE before striving to be EFFICIENT'.

PRODUCTIVITY

Productivity is very often confused with efficiency and effectiveness. Though related, all the three terms carry different meanings.

Efficiency (η) is the ratio of actual output attained to the standard expected output. Therefore, efficiency indicates a measure of how well the resources are utilised to accomplish a target or result. In the above example, if the crew is expected to produce 2,000 widgets per day and they produce 1,800 they are 90% efficient.

Effectiveness (Ø): it is the degree of accomplishing the objectives.

Therefore, effectiveness indicates a measure of how well a set of targets or results are accomplished. Again, if the sales of widgets are 10,000 per week and the factory produces 10,000 then it is 100% effective.

Productivity is an integration of both efficiency and effectiveness. It indicates a combined effect of resource utilisation (efficiency) and performance (effectiveness). The combined effect of efficiency and effectiveness is used in defining a term called productivity. Productivity has by implication a people element and one measure of productivity which has become popular is also known as Labour Efficiency.

Labour Efficiency or Productivity

Measuring labour efficiency is the starting point for raising productivity since it calculates how well we are using our manpower resources. Let us consider, once again, the widget operation. Recalling that each person produces 400 widgets per day and assuming he or she is working on the widget machine for 8 hours each day, then they produce 50 widgets per hour. We can look at this in a different way. For every 50 widgets produced, we recover 1 'man' hour. (Excuse the politically incorrect metric.)

Although we have calculated that he or she works for 8 hours, we know they must have a break sometime during the shift. Let us assume that he or she has a half an hour lunch break and two

47

15 minute tea breaks, for which they are paid. The total 'manned hours paid', therefore, is 8 + 0.5 + 2 x 0.25 = 9.0 hours.

Let us define productivity (or Labour Efficiency) as:

Productivity = <u>Man-Hours Recovered at Standard</u> x 100%
Total manned hours paid

If we consider the whole crew of five persons (before the efficiency drive), for a daily production of 2,000 widgets, the calculation of productivity is:

Productivity = 100 x (2000 divided by 50) /5 x 9

= 100 x 40/45 = 88.89%

You might ask, so what? Well, for a start, when the sales director is calculating the price to sell the widgets for, he is assuming a rate of 500 widgets for every hour the operator is paid. He does not allow for the rest time when no widgets are produced. To recover the full expenditure on salaries, he has to assume that each worker only produces 400 x 0.8889 widgets per PAID hour.

If the machine making the widgets stops and starts, then during the downtime there is also no labour recovery. For machinery, the measurement of productivity can, therefore, be quite complex.

For manufacturing industries, labour efficiency is very important and its measurement is the key to improving output. This, however, is beyond the scope of this module. I would recommend for anyone who wishes to learn more to read the excellent book, 'Productivity and how to measure it' by Andrew Wilson. (Lulu Publications)

Overall Equipment Effectiveness

Another measure, normally associated with lean enterprises, is Overall Equipment Effectiveness (OEE). As the name suggests, it looks at a number of elements that contribute to efficiency. It is a total measure of performance that relates the availability of the process to productivity and quality.

To understand the importance of OEE, let us consider a situation where we are told that our department is running flat out. We might reasonably assume that the equipment is running efficiently and effectively, but what if the equipment only runs for 75% of the time? What if when it is running it runs at 80% of its speed? What if only 90% of the parts it makes are good? Individually these performance measures may appear to indicate an acceptable piece of equipment, but is it a true picture?

To answer this, we need to understand what is impacting on these performance figures. Let us define OEE as:

AVAILABILITY x PRODUCTIVITY x QUALITY

In the above example the Overall Equipment Effectiveness is:

0.75 x 0.80 x 0.90 = 54%

There are six big loses that impact on the performance of a piece of equipment and reduce its output significantly. These shown graphically below:

OEE and the Six Big Losses

Equipment	Six Big Losses
Total Available time	Planned Downtime
Available time	1 Breakdowns
	2 Setup / adjustment
Available operating time	3 Idling / minor stoppages
Actual operating time	4 Speed
Effective operating time	5 Defects in process and rework
	6 Start up losses

Losses one to three may seem self-evident. I remember the sales pitch an injection moulding machine supplier once made to me. The salesman said he would be happy to give me a written guarantee for his machine. 'I guarantee,' he continued with his pitch, 'that it will break down!' The 'punch line' was that it would not be very often and when it did, he would ensure first class service. It was an easy guarantee. Machines, however reliable, do break down (Loss 1). They also require setting-up and running adjustments (Loss 2). There may also be many minor stoppages that are often missed with manual downtime recording systems. This is one area that can often generate quick-win productivity improvements.

In the eighties, I ran a company that operated, amongst other equipment, a number of silk-screen printing machines. These were loaded and unloaded manually by the operator and appeared to run reasonably smoothly. Although the manual downtime reporting system showed few stoppages, overall output was always well below what was expected from the reported downtime figures.

I introduced an automatic downtime recording system called Dextrolog where any stoppage was automatically recorded and measured. I was amazed to find out how many stoppages occurred which were under two minutes. Conventional manual recording systems often ignore short stoppages. When the operators were asked to explain the reason for this, they explained that the ink on the screens often began to dry out, causing poor print quality. They would have to stop the machine and give the silk-screen a quick wipe with a cloth coated in a solvent. Although, in itself, each stoppage did not seem significant, in total 18% of the available time was being lost to cleaning the screens. More importantly, none of this downtime was recorded by the operators! Once this was realised, it was simply a matter of adding a retarder to the ink to stop it drying too quickly.

The next loss, speed, (number 3) can also have a significant impact on OEE. Often, if a machine is giving intermittent problems, the operator or technician will reduce the speed to 'settle it down'. On first consideration, it might appear a 'no-brainer.' Keeping the machine running steadily is much less disruptive than a stop-start operation. Unless the reasons for stop-start are quickly resolved, however, slowing the machine may also be as detrimental to output. Operators are satisfied to keep the machine running but of course, a 10% reduction in speed is a straight 10% drop in output.

So, after the first four losses are absorbed, we may be forgiven for thinking that everything else is plain sailing. Not so. Every product that is rejected (Loss 5) is a loss of productive time. People often forget this, particularly if the rejection of product comes later. Finally, starting a machine after changeover can often cause defective products (Loss 6) that must be accounted for in the effective operating time.

As a post-script to our discussions on metrics, it is wise to remember that, as a general rule THE THINGS THAT WE MEASURE WILL IMPROVE. Now we have an understanding of the metrics we can put in place to assess our progress, let us now turn to the tools and techniques we can use to smooth our journey.

MODULE 3

PROBLEM SOLVING TEAMS

If we are to be successful in our quest to be World Class, we know that we will face problems that must be overcome. It is important to remember that all problems are overcomeable. The solutions and their implementation, however, are only fully achieved by involving those directly involved in the processes. When I worked as a lean consultant, my role was not to be the knight on the white charger charging in to fight the dragon of mediocrity with my superior knowledge of lean. Any improvements that might result would quickly evaporate as people rejected the new regime imposed on them, and drifted, albeit slowly, back to their old ways of working. My role was to work patiently with key employees, training them in lean principles and then taking a back seat as they applied their learning. As I said in the introduction, the principal barrier to implementing lean successfully involves changing people's mindsets and behaviours. Employee Involvement (EI) is the key to changing mindsets.

One way of achieving this is through the training process. By training people on the principles of lean and then forming them into problem-solving teams, a truly effective lean culture will develop.

Problem-solving teams, either Corrective Action Teams (CATs) or alternatively called Continuous Improvement Teams (CIT) are the key to our success. The elements of lean revealed in this book provide a basic introduction to anyone who wishes to join such a team, giving a practical understanding of lean and its tools and techniques.

Let us be clear what constitutes a problem-solving team. It is a group of individuals assembled to work on a project that involves resolving issues that have either arisen or are likely to arise. Typically it will be formed for a limited period of time and will include staff from different parts of the organisation with the relevant skill sets.

To be effective, team members need to have skills in problem-solving techniques and knowledge of producing SOPs. If team members do not already possess these skills, a short training course should be undertaken. If we are going to impose STABILITY within our organisation, we need to establish 'Best Practice' in every area and then capture it. We will consider SOPs later. Before we can write an SOP, however, we need to ensure that we have resolved outstanding problems with the process. So how do we define a problem?

WHAT IS A PROBLEM?

We could fool ourselves, if we wish, by saying that we spend most of our waking day solving problems. The subject of problem-solving is a book in its own right, so let me speed up this introduction by saying, most of the time, when we think we are solving problems, we are actually making choices.

For example, what should we eat for dinner? It might appear to be a problem, but in reality, it is usually making a choice from the items we have available to us. To understand this, let us first consider the problem of 'what is a problem?'

There are many definitions, but in business terms, let us define a problem as:

'A gap between a perceived state and a desired state'

So, for example, when I look into my garden I see an abundance of vegetation mingled with a glorious confusion of colours. As I enjoy its rugged beauty I think everything is fine.

No problem! The view matches my perception of the perfect garden and, to me, no actions are required.

My neighbour, however, looks over his garden wall and is appalled! Instead of the neat rows of flower beds surrounding an immaculate lawn, he perceives a wilderness of weeds and untamed desolation. In his mind, there is a gap between the perceived state and the desired state. He definitely sees a problem to be solved.

The key word in our definition is perception, or how we interpret what we are seeing. In management reporting and control systems, perception is less of an issue. In our OEE analysis, for example, it may be that we allow a planned machine downtime of 5%. If actual downtime is 4%, then no action is required. There is no gap to eliminate and therefore, in theory, we do not have a problem. If it is 6%, however, there is a gap of 1% and we need to take action.

So, if we now have a definition of what constitutes a problem, let us look at the process of solving problems. It is, in fact, a seven-step process:

Define the problem

Collect data and information

Analyse the data

Propose solutions

Sense-check solutions and decide

Install the solution

Implement the solution

Having said this, it is amazing how many people think it is a two-stage process:

Decide solution – Install solution

Without any thought as to what the actual problem is, many people have a tendency to 'jump in with both feet' confusing activity with action. Albert Einstein once said,

"If I had 60 minutes to save the world, I would spend the first 55 minutes, defining the problem"

A little like the pilot who told us he didn't know where he was and where he was heading but was going as fast as he could, unless we know exactly what problem we are trying to solve, our actions might even be counter-productive. Of the seven-step process, defining the problem and implementing the solution are the two critical steps. Most people consider that once the solution is installed, the problem is solved. This is often not the case and the most common reason for the solution eventually failing. Implementing the solution means ensuring that it is understood by everyone involved and it is embedded in the daily routines of the department and carried out by all. Remember:

The principle barrier to implementing lean successfully involves changing people's mindsets and behaviours

We will look at techniques for ensuring compliance with the agreed solution by our team members when we consider Leading4Lean in Book 3.

DEFINING THE PROBLEM

Whenever I ran this part of the programme in a training course, I always asked the delegates to watch a short cartoon showing Sylvester the Cat trying to catch Tweety Pie, a yellow canary. For those of a different generation who are wondering what on earth I am talking about, these were two cartoon characters perpetually at war with each other in the same vein as Tom and Gerry who I am sure you will have heard of. Sylvester was for every coming up with imaginative ways to catch Tweety Pie who sat smugly and securely in his gilded cage.

When I asked the delegates what problem Sylvester was trying to solve the answer was usually along the lines that he was trying to find the best way to catch Tweety Pie. When I asked why he wanted to catch him, the answer was usually, to eat of course! Since the purpose of the exercise was to help them focus on defining the problem, their thought processes began to shift from trying to find the best way of catching Tweety Pie towards how Sylvester might satisfy his appetite.

This leads us to the fundamental step in defining a problem, writing a **problem statement**.

A problem statement is a clear concise description of the issue(s) that need(s) to be addressed by the problem-solving team. It is used to focus the team at the beginning of the project, keep them on track and to validate that the team delivered an outcome that solves the problem statement.

The University of Sheffield offers good advice on writing a problem statement and I make no apologies for displaying it below:

What?

A problem statement is usually one or two sentences to explain the problem your process improvement project will address. In general, a problem statement will outline the negative points of the current situation and explain why this matters. It also serves as a great communication tool, helping to get buy-in and support from others.

Why?

One of the most important goals of any problem statement is to define the problem being addressed in a way that's clear and precise. Its aim is to focus the process improvement team's activities and steer the scope of the project.

How?

Creation of a problem statement is an activity that is best completed in a small group (4-6 people). It is helpful to have a couple of people who are involved in the process and a process owner involved in the activity.

1. Get each person to write his or her own problem statement without conferring. Compare each of the sentences/ looking for common themes and wording.

2. Start to write an improved statement using the common themes.

3. Ensure that the problems include the customer's perspective

4. Ensure that the statement focuses on existing problems.

5. Try to include the time frame over which the problem has been occurring.

6. Try to quantify the problem. If you do not have the data to hand, defer writing the final problem statement until you have been able to quantify the problem.

You should be able to apply the 5 'W's (Who, What, Where, When and Why) to the problem statement. *(We will discuss this technique later)* A problem statement can be refined as you start to further investigate the root cause.

Finally, review your new problem statement against the following criteria:

- It should focus on only one problem.
- It should be one or two sentences long.
- It should not suggest a solution.

An example problem statement:

The staffing model in the Process Improvement Unit (PIU) has changed (we have more staff and some of the staff have different working patterns) we need to have a clear way of recording status and stage of our business activities (projects, workshops and training) that will be used by all PIU staff, so that we can work effectively and provide good service to our customers. A member of staff is due to go on annual leave in two weeks time and we have no visibility or way of easily sharing information about their work, this will make it hard for the rest of the team to cover the work during staff absence.

As you can see from this well-thought-out problem statement, it keeps the team on track throughout the project.

On the same theme, I wrote a problem definition statement for our local church when we received a letter from the National Park telling us that the roof lights installed by our contractor in one of the church properties were in breach of regulations. To help focus our efforts, I defined the problem as:

'To work with the Exmoor National Park Authority and our architect to resolve the issue of a breach in the planning application for 3 & 4 Church Lane in respect of the flush fitting of the conservative style roof lights. To ensure the costs of rectifying the problem are borne by those responsible for the breach and at minimum cost to the church. To ensure the implementation of the solution is done with the minimum of disruption to the tenants. To maintain the goodwill of all parties involved throughout the exercise.'

By having clarity at the start, the issue was resolved successfully at no cost to the church.

THE SEVEN TOOLS OF QUALITY

Once we have decided what the problem is, the next stage of the process is to collect data so we can analyse it. This is where the Seven Tools of Quality come in, which I summarise below.

THE SEVEN TOOLS OF QUALITY

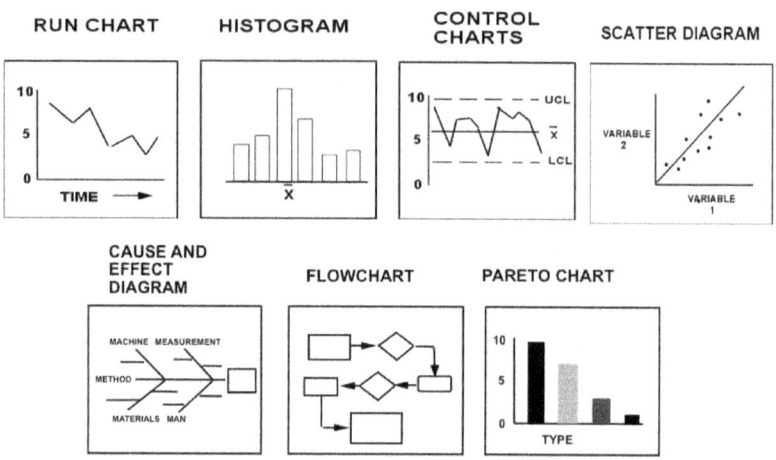

I have shown the seven tools diagrammatically and I am sure that many of you may be familiar with them already. Below I give a brief description of each tool together with examples as to when we might use them.

60

Run Chart

A run chart is where we collect data and plot it on a chart. Often this is the value of a variable we wish to control as the y-axis (vertical line) with time as the x-axis (horizontal line.) For example, let us consider a bottling machine that is filling 1L shampoo bottles. The variation in fill volume with time is shown below:

Filling 1L bottles of a shampoo

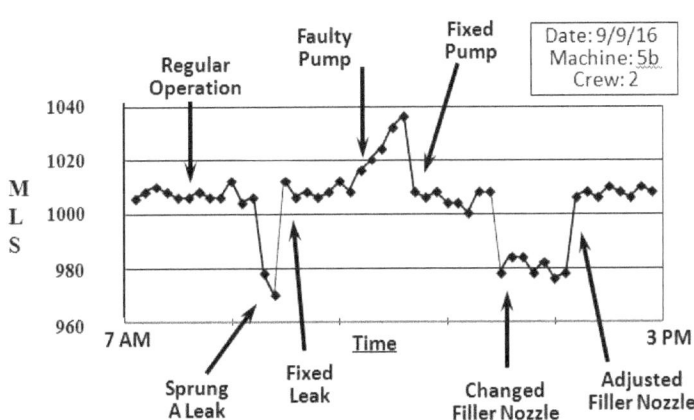

From the chart, we can get a picture of what is happening in our process. It is clear that there are times of variability which have a common cause. For the process shown, it is from about 07:00 – 09:00 and then from 13:30 – 15:00 hours. We can highlight specific events during the run and identify the specific causes. We can then decide what we need to do to eliminate them. Run charts are often the first step in identifying the problems in the process.

Histogram

If we were to plot the above data as a histogram or bar chart, the pattern would not be as clear. A Histogram is an effective

61

way to organise data. Instead of looking at a table or list of points, we make a picture that shows how the points are "distributed" (i.e. where they are located on the scale)

Consider the annual snowfall in the mythical kingdom of Camelot. The 'raw' data is shown below:

"It Just Doesn't Snow Around Here Like It Used To"

1958-59	357.1	1974-75	231.6	1990-91	178.0
1959-60	410.7	1975-76	218.9	1991-92	299.7
1960-91	227.1	1976-77	233.9	1992-93	334.0
1961-62	166.6	1977-78	408.7	1993-94	320.5
1962-63	194.0	1978-79	351.8	1994-95	142.2
1963-64	233.7	1979-80	183.4	1995-96	331.0
1964-65	180.6	1980-81	239.8	1996-97	265.9
1965-66	262.1	1981-82	326.1	1997-98	253.5
1966-67	188.0	1982-83	152.1	1998-99	273.8
1967-68	194.6	1983-84	299.7	1999-00	283.5
1968-69	202.7	1984-85	221.2	2000-01	336.6
1969-70	303.8	1985-86	179.6	2001-02	146.0
1970-71	362.4	1986-87	170.4	2002-03	
1971-72	267.0	1987-88	165.6	2003-04	
1972-73	185.4	1988-89	220.0	2004-05	
1974-74	253.2	1989-90	268.7	2005-06	

The data in itself is not very helpful in showing us what rainfall we might expect. To make more sense of this, we need to analyse the data in a different way. Rather than thinking in terms individual values of the rainfall, we need to group similar numbers into a limited number of rainfall 'ranges'. In this case, let us set the interval for each range at 50 cm. Next, we need to identify the lowest snowfall which, from the table, is 146 cm. To be sure that we can capture future data, let us start our scale, the x-axis, at 130 cm. Remembering that we have set our interval at 50 cm, we now count the number of instances where the snowfall was between 130 cm and 180 cm. In the example, this is 8. This figure is plotted on the y-axis of the histogram.

Next, we count the number of instances where the snowfall was in the range 180.01 to 230 cm. From the data, we can see there are 11 occasions when snowfall was between these two levels. And so we continue until all the data has been covered in the ranges we selected. At the completion of our analysis we can generate the following histogram where the x-axis is the ranges we identified and the y-axis the number of occurrences:

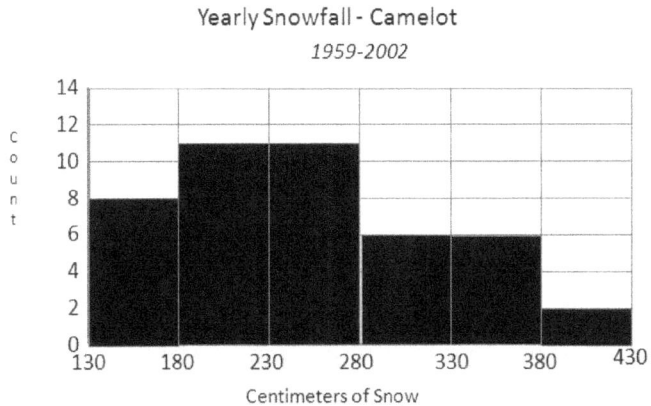

Here we can see that, while there are some years with low snowfalls, and some years where Camelot is overwhelmed, most of the time we can expect snowfalls between 180 and 280 cm. (We should not confuse histograms with bar charts where, although the x-axis is still defined by intervals, the y-axis is the actual value itself and not the number of occurrences.)

So, how do we use this new-found knowledge? Let us go back to filling out 1L bottles again. Analysing data from the filling process as a histogram gives the following chart:

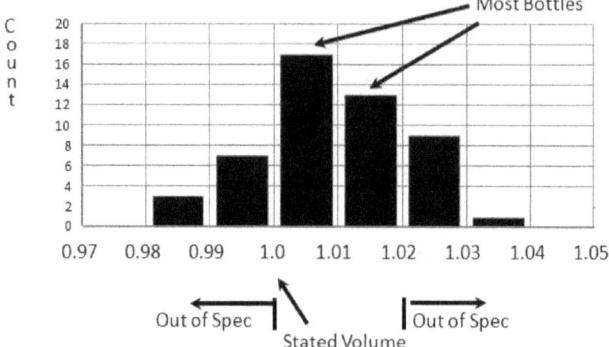

Filling 1 liter bottles of shampoo(Spec = 1.0 - 1.02 l.)

I have added the manufacturing specification set by the customer (1.00 – 1.02 L) to the chart. Whilst the majority of bottles are in specification, it is clear that whilst some bottles have been overfilled, others are below specification. Clearly, the process is not capable of filling bottles within this range.

Control Charts

A Control chart is a tool for decision-making. It helps distinguish between common and special cause variation and uses statistically derived limits based on data from the process.

Like a run chart, it plots the variation of one parameter with time. Superimposed onto the chart, however, are the upper and lower limits of the parameter that are allowed by the process specification. Between the upper and lower limits, a centre line is shown. In the example above, the filled volume of the shampoo was specified between 1.00 and 1.20 L. The centre line would, therefore, be 1.10 L.

An example is shown below. In this case, despite the variations, the parameter remains within the agreed specification.

64

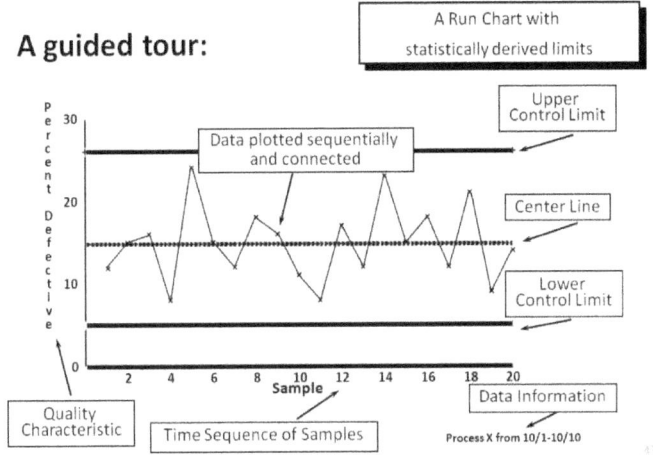

A guided tour:

A Run Chart with statistically derived limits

When there is variation within the natural variability of the process, it is known as a common cause variant. When it goes outside the normal process variability, it is known as a special cause variant. Consider a process that is showing common cause variation that begins to drift outside the control parameters. The process, for some reason, has gone from being predictable and stable to being unstable and out of control.

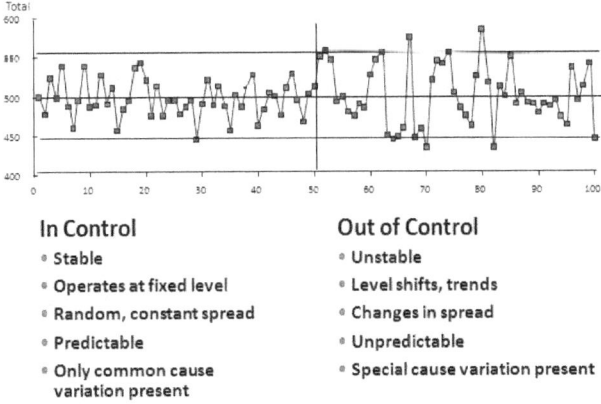

In Control
- Stable
- Operates at fixed level
- Random, constant spread
- Predictable
- Only common cause variation present

Out of Control
- Unstable
- Level shifts, trends
- Changes in spread
- Unpredictable
- Special cause variation present

65

Control charts are used to signal when action is required. As a rule:

- When only <u>Common Causes</u> present:
- Do not react to individual data points.
- Improvements require changes to the system.
- When <u>Special Causes</u> are present:

Take action - the action required will depend on the situation. We can use either:

Corrective Action Guidelines (CAG's) or

Analytical Trouble Shooting to provide the path forward.

Let us look what happens when we respond, as people often do, to common cause variations. Consider the thermostat in your house, assuming you have central heating. It is a simple form of controller. When the temperature drops to a certain temperature, the thermostat calls for action and the boiler kicks in. Once the temperature reaches the upper limit set by the designers, the thermostat signals for the boiler to stop. The upper chart shown below shows the natural cycle of the system. The lower limit is 67 degrees and the upper limit 69 degrees.

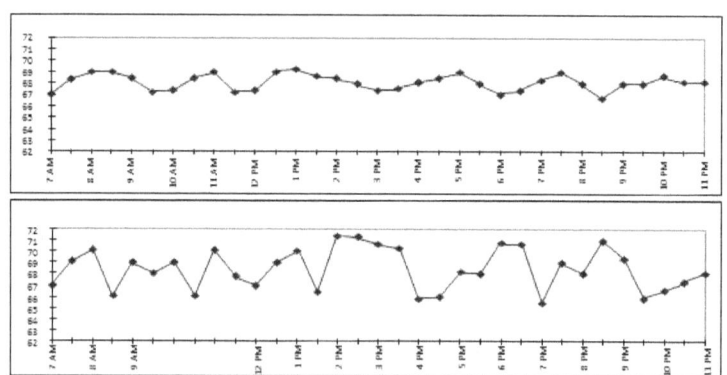

What happens if we interfere with the natural system and take action when it is not required? The lower chart shows what happens. Instead of a gently cycling system, we now have a system which is unstable.

Although this is a simple example and depicts a situation which is unlikely to occur, taking action for common cause variations happens frequently.

When I was the manufacturing manager of a plastics packaging company, the MD appointed a new Quality Manager. In her enthusiasm to improve the quality of the products, she decided to tighten the weight specifications for the containers we produced. Not understanding the processes, she set the upper and lower weight limits too tight such that they were beyond the capability of the injection moulding machines. The result was chaos! Operators were adjusting moulding parameters after every sample measurement. The result was similar to the thermostat; the variations became wider, not tighter as she had planned and quality dropped as rejections soared.

The key, of course, is to conduct a process capability study to determine the upper and lower limits to determine the common cause variants. Once these are known, by using the control chart, the secondary checks, such as weight are, in theory, unnecessary and only made to confirm product quality meets specification. This is known as Statistical Process Control (SPC) and is a key ingredient in lean and world class manufacturing.

Scatter Diagram

A Scatter Plot shows the relationship between two variables. For example, the chart below shows that as children get taller, they weigh more. Each point on the plot represents an individual child for which a pair of measurements (height and weight) are available. The question is: "Are the height and weight-related?"

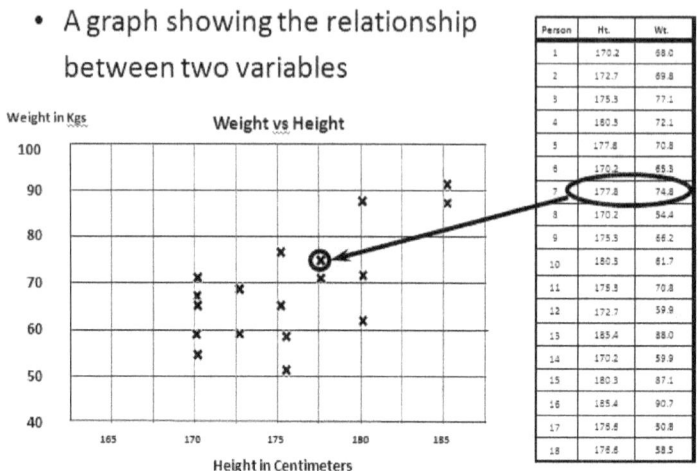

- A graph showing the relationship between two variables

Weight vs Height

Person	Ht.	Wt.
1	170.2	88.0
2	172.7	69.8
3	175.3	77.1
4	180.3	72.1
5	177.8	70.8
6	170.2	65.3
7	177.8	74.8
8	170.2	54.4
9	175.3	66.2
10	180.3	81.7
11	175.3	70.8
12	172.7	59.9
13	185.4	88.0
14	170.2	59.9
15	180.3	87.1
16	185.4	90.7
17	175.6	50.8
18	176.6	58.5

A Run Chart is a special case of a Scatter Plot where the horizontal axis is time. In a Run Chart, the question is "How does a variable (on the vertical axis) change over time (on the horizontal axis)?". In a Scatter Plot, the question is "How does one variable (on the vertical axis) change as another variable (on the horizontal axis) changes?"

These are the elements of a Scatter Plot: The horizontal axis (X-Axis) is the INDEPENDENT or PREDICTOR variable. The vertical axis (Y-Axis) is the variable that DEPENDS on, or whose value you want to PREDICT using the X-axis variable. The plotted point (X, Y) are two measures on the same individual or experimental unit.

The label or identification should completely identify the data, when it was collected, and where. This could be a title, a legend box or both. Be sure to include all pertinent information such as machine, shift, etc.

Let us look at an example of a test on cockroach poison at different dosage levels:

- Each point (x,y) represents an x (dose) and a y (roaches killed) in one test

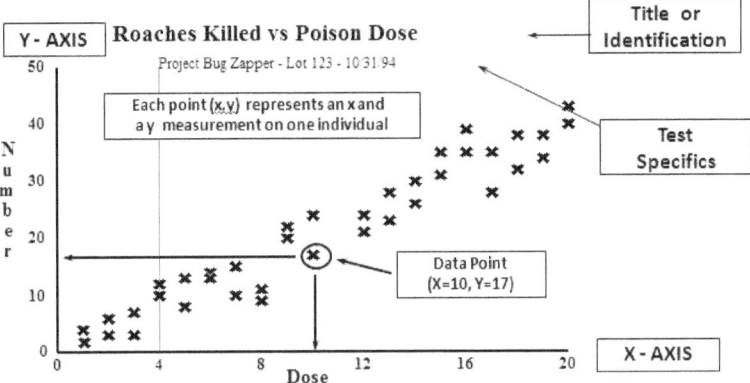

The Y-axis shows the number of cockroaches killed at each dose of poison tested. As you might expect, the larger the dose the more cockroaches are killed.

Here are some examples of scatter plots that show the relationship between two variables. Note that these need not be cause and effect relationships.

69

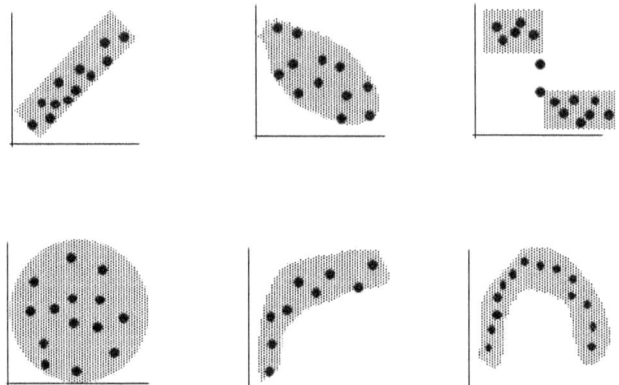

Top Left: a strong positive (as one variable goes up, so does the other) relationship. There is little variability. Examples:
 - Yield in a process vs. temperature
 - Volume of water pumped vs. valve setting

Top Middle: a weak negative relationship (one goes down as the other goes up). It has a lot of scatter (variability), possibly due to other factors or variables. Examples:
 - Picture quality vs. temperature at which a film is stored
 - Sales of movie tickets vs. cost of groceries

Top Right: Two groups of data where no relationship appears within the groups. Examples:
 - Babies born vs. income in two different cities
 - Percent defects vs. machine speed on two different machines

Bottom Left: No relationship what so ever. Examples:
 - Lottery numbers drawn vs. fortune teller's predictions
 - Sales of chewing gum vs. sunspot activity

Bottom Middle: There is a strong positive relationship, but the variable on the vertical axis has a maximum.

.

70

Examples:
- Height vs. age
- Percent of bacteria killed vs. dose of medicine

Bottom Right: There is a strong relationship, positive at first, but then negative after a maximum is reached. Examples:
- Hours studied vs. grade achieved on a test (reversal due to lack of sleep)
- Flavour rating of a stew vs. amount of spice (reversal due to too much spice)

Selecting the Axis

When choosing the X and Y axis, it is important to remember that the independent variable should be on the X-axis. By this, I mean it should be the "cause" in cause and effect situations or the "predictor" in prediction situations. For example, if we believe there is a correlation between the temperature in a chemical reaction and the yield, then the X-axis should be temperature. The Y-axis is then the dependent variable i.e. the "effect" in cause and effect situations or the "predicted" in prediction situations. In other words, if we believe higher temperature is the cause of higher yield (the effect), then we should plot the variables as shown below:

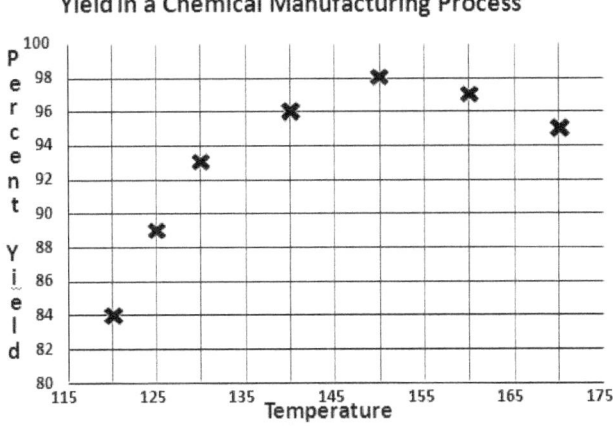

71

Cause and Effect Diagram.

Often called a Fishbone Chart because of its shape, this is a very useful tool for getting to the bottom of a problem and helps us focus on the areas that require action, including collecting data. Whilst it can be used by an individual, it is best used as a brainstorming technique in a problem-solving team. To be successful, there should be little discussion about individual issues as they are listed. The idea is to capture, on paper or a whiteboard, all the elements that may contribute to the non-compliance or 'problem'.

Usually, the areas considered are the five M's – Materials, Machines Manning, Measurement, and Methods, as these are common elements in most instances of non-compliance. Others can be added, for example, Environment. All the items that might contribute to the problem are listed under one or more of these headings. The key is to list all the items first and not try to eliminate any. I give an example below:

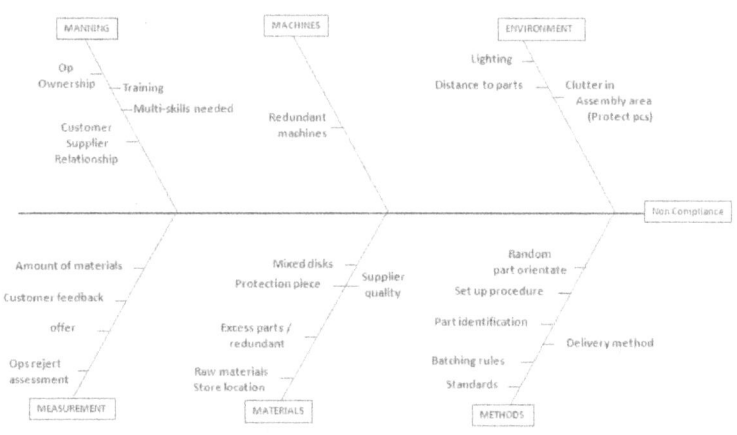

In the example, someone considers that the problem may be related to lack of skills of the operators. Under Manning, therefore, we have added Training. This then throws up the option of multi-skilling the operators as a possible solution.

Once all the elements which may affect the problem are listed, the team can then prioritise the ones to investigate. A useful technique for getting to the root cause of a problem is called the 'five whys.'

The Five Whys

We simply ask the question 'Why' when we have a none-compliance. For example, consider a machine that has stopped unexpectedly. Let us assume the overload has tripped out. The temptation is to reset the overload, or worse, increase the overload setting.

When we ask the question 'why' did the overload trip, we realise that there is insufficient oil on the shaft. Again, the temptation might be to add oil to the crankcase.

When we ask the question 'why' was there insufficient oil, we realise that the oil pump is inefficient. Do we need a new oil pump? When we ask the question 'why' again, we realise that it is inefficient because the pump drive shaft is worn. Why is it worn? The fifth 'why' leads us to the answer, the oil filter is BLOCKED with swarf! At last, we have discovered the root-cause of the problem.

Q : WHY has machine stopped ?   **Q** : WHY overload trip ?   **Q** : WHY Insufficient oil ?
A : Overload tripped out !   **A** : Insufficient oil on shaft !   **A** : Oil pump inefficient !

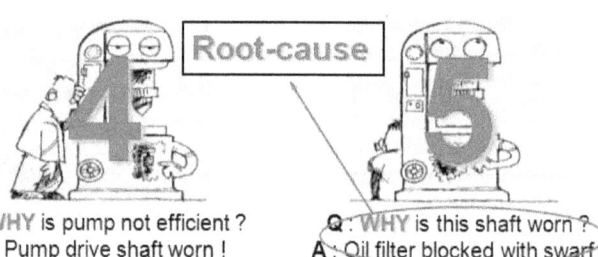

Q : WHY is pump not efficient ?   **Q** : WHY is this shaft worn ?
A : Pump drive shaft worn !   **A** : Oil filter blocked with swarf !

Fishbone charts are an effective way of helping us resolve problems with the process. Ironically, in the above example, had we introduced TPM and placed the oil filter cleaning on a regular maintenance schedule, we could have avoided the problem and saved the cost of lost production and a new pump shaft.

The following diagram shows how to put together a cause and effect diagram:

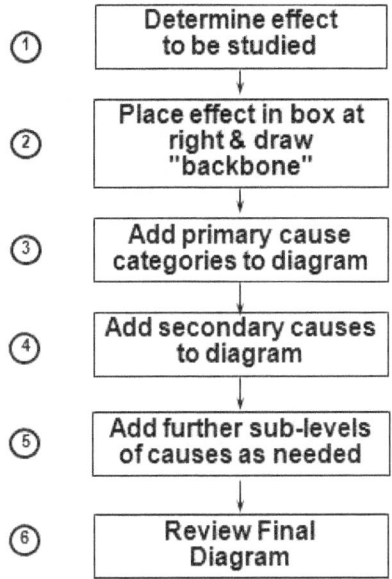

Depending on the nature of the organisation, standard categories can be chosen in terms specific to the area of application. For example, in the 5 'M's instead of "machine", a more appropriate term might be "rewinder" or "slitter".

The **5M's** (Machine, Manpower, Method, Materials, Measurement) are most often used when dealing with manufacturing related problems.

•The **4P's** (Policies, Procedure, People, Plant) are often used in conjunction with service or administrative problems.

•The **5W's** (Who, What, When, Where, Why) are used with any type of troubleshooting.

If when deciding on the areas to consider you get more than **4-6 major categories** you might think about combining similar categories into one larger grouping for ease of understanding.

75

Flowcharts

A flowchart is a diagram that describes a sequence of operations. By breaking the process into its individual operations, the waste can be identified. Symbols are used to represent the operations and these are shown below:

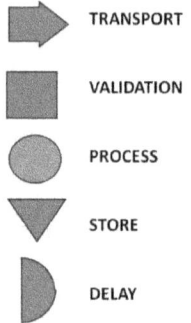

TRANSPORT

VALIDATION

PROCESS

STORE

DELAY

The processing operation is shown as a green circle. It is coloured 'green' to signify this is the only time that we add value to the product. Everything else constitutes waste and is shown in red. As an example, let us look how we might generate a process flowchart within a payroll office. The first stage is to identify each step in producing the product which in this case is a computerised timesheet record in order to calculate pay.

Dept : Payroll   Activity : Timesheets

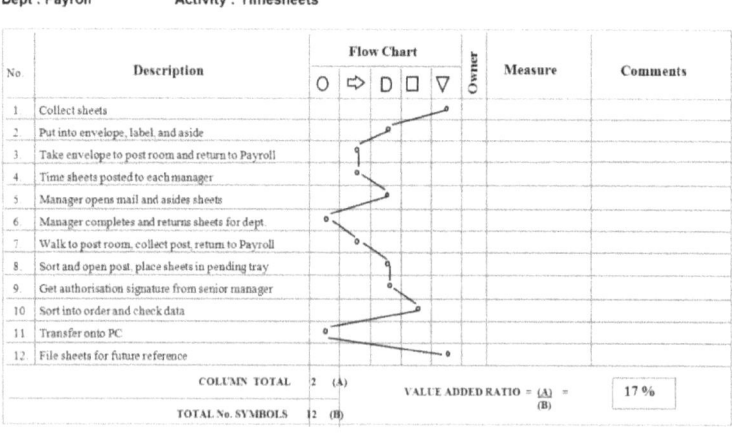

No.	Description	Flow Chart					Owner	Measure	Comments
		O	⇨	D	☐	▽			
1	Collect sheets								
2	Put into envelope, label, and aside								
3	Take envelope to post room and return to Payroll								
4	Time sheets posted to each manager								
5	Manager opens mail and asides sheets								
6	Manager completes and returns sheets for dept.								
7	Walk to post room, collect post, return to Payroll								
8	Sort and open post, place sheets in pending tray								
9	Get authorisation signature from senior manager								
10	Sort into order and check data								
11	Transfer onto PC								
12	File sheets for future reference								

COLUMN TOTAL   2   (A)

TOTAL No. SYMBOLS   12   (B)

VALUE ADDED RATIO $= \frac{(A)}{(B)} =$ | 17 % |

We start by looking at each step and deciding whether it is processing, transport, delay, validation or store. We can then calculate the percentage of time we are adding value in the process. In this case, it is 17% which is not unusual and possibly on the high side! The next step is to look at opportunities to reduce waste by cutting out some of the steps. By doing so we are likely to reduce the time taken to process the timesheet. (This is usually called the cycle time).

In this example, the end result is a validated and authorised computerised file. One option to reduce waste is to collect the data electronically in the first instance and then distribute it for validation and authorisation. This does not require a bespoke computer system, we could simply input the information into an excel spreadsheet and email the document to the interested parties. Once the new way of working is decided, the next stage in the process is to capture this in a Standard Operating Procedure. (SOP). Flowcharts can be used as part of an SOP to illustrate the steps required, as in the following example:

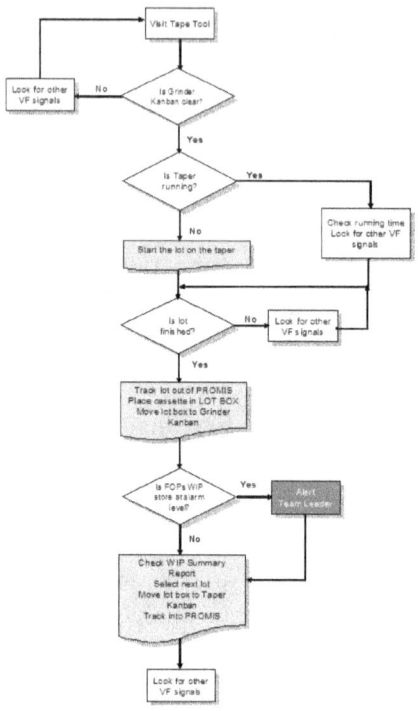

Pareto Chart

A Pareto Chart is a statistical technique used in decision making. It stems from what is known as the Pareto Principle. Pareto was an Italian economist who noted that 20% of the people controlled 80% of the wealth. This is the origin of the 80/20 rule you may have heard of.

Another way of expressing this is that 20% of the effort produces 80% of the result. For example, in the game of cricket, 80% of the runs are often scored by 20% of the batsmen.

The advantage of using the Pareto Principle stretches into many diverse areas. When I was appointed business manager of a federation of three schools, one of my primary tasks was to reduce the non-teaching expenses. Rather than taking a piecemeal approach, I conducted a Pareto analysis on federation expenditure and identified the top 20% of items that contributed to 80% of the spend. In this way, I reduced the number of items I had to focus on from 50 down to 10 and was able to quickly make a dramatic reduction in costs.

When constructing a Pareto chart, tally sheets are often used. Tally sheets are a simple way of collecting data on a process as it occurs. Any type of defect or occurrence can be captured on a tally sheet. Pareto diagrams are then used to help sort the data by order of importance. An example of a tally chart or check sheet investigating the reasons for being late for work is shown below:

Reasons for Being Late to Work

Check Sheet		
Traffic	I	1
Long Wait at Light	III	3
Bathroom Hang Up	IIII IIII II	12
Breakfast Hang Up	II	2
Weather	II II	4
Car Problems	I	1
Clock Disagrees	II	2

The possible causes of the problem, in this case, lateness, are first identified and added to the left column of the chart. As each instance of lateness occurs, a stroke is added against the reason. The convention is that the fifth stroke is made diagonally across the others to make counting in units of five easy.

We can now rearrange the data in descending order to create the Pareto Chart:

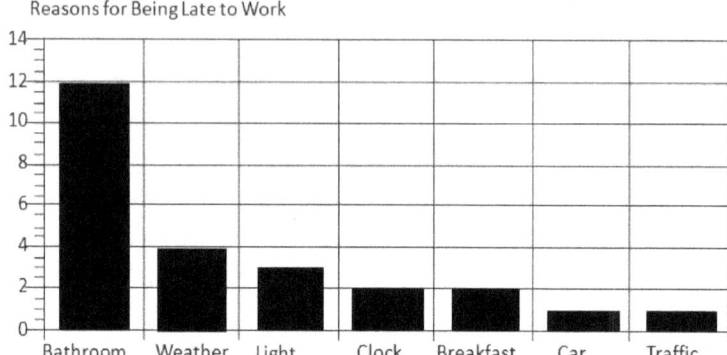
Reasons for Being Late to Work

Clearly, if the person in the above example wishes to improve his or her attendance, getting into the bathroom early is the one item directly in their control.

Pareto charts can be developed to highlight problems which, when resolved, will have the biggest impact on performance. Tally charts and Pareto Diagrams are particularly useful when analysing the short and frequent stoppages we considered when discussing OEE.

MODULE 4

STANDARD OPERATIONS

Henry Ford, the father of mass production techniques once said, "Give a lazy man an easy job and he'll find an easier way of doing it!" No doubt the lazy man was breaking the task down into its component parts and taking out the wasted steps, arrived at an easier way of working. Once this method has been identified, no doubt it would have been incorporated into an SOP. Our definition of a Standard Operation is:

A Standard Operation is centred around human movements, outlining efficient, safe working methods that eliminate waste whilst ensuring proper use of equipment and tooling.

Standard operations are used for training of staff, as a means of standardisation as well as a platform for improvements. They can also be used to identify and record safe working practices and are a tool to help manage the work-place. They act as an audit document to check that a person is actually performing the operation in the safest and most efficient way.

When I worked as Federation Business Manager, I introduced SOPs into the admin departments of the three schools. The initial reaction of the staff was incredibility. To me, the need was obvious. If one of the staff members was off ill in one school for example, by having SOPs in that department, a member of staff from another school could go to the school and perform the task. The normal method was to wait until the person came back to work. This meant that purchasing requests could remain unprocessed for days or even weeks.

After some initial reluctance, the advantage of SOPs became obvious to the team. Compiling the monthly financial report was a laborious and time-consuming task. In one of the schools, a newly appointed finance officer struggled to meet the deadline.

By getting a long-serving finance officer from another school to write the SOP, the task became clearer and therefore easier. Any initial resistance within the team faded and they embraced SOPs as a good way of working.

In one school, the automatic doors operated by the security system would periodically fail. The caretaker from another school would have to be called to reset them. Magically he would resolve the problem and then disappear, leaving the staff no wiser as to what he had done. Having introduced the staff to SOPs, they asked to sit down with the caretaker and list the steps and the decision-making required to reset the doors. This allowed them to produce an SOP. Once all the staff members were trained in this method, the mystery and magic disappeared and they no longer had to wait for the caretaker to appear to reset the security door.

When I finally left the federation, amongst my leaving presents from my team was a bottle of wine with an SOP on how to open and then drink it!

Developing an SOP

To develop the Standard Operating Procedure the first step is to select the operation to be recorded. If, for example, it is a production process, then most likely there will be data regarding this; for instance, cycle time which is the time to produce one unit.

The second step is to record all the available data for the process. This will allow us to measure any improvements we make.

Next, we can analyse the operation by gathering all the relevant paperwork and ensuring all parts and tooling are at hand. If the operation is done by others, we should watch it being performed and if it a shift operation, watch it across all shifts where possible. It is important to ask the operators for their inputs as these are usually the people who have the best ideas as to how the operation might be improved. It may be that the operations are performed in a particular sequence and we should try and identify this, taking rough notes throughout our analysis.

Once we have gathered the information as to how the process is currently undertaken, the next step is to develop the best method of carrying it out. If it is done over a number of shifts, we should ask if there are differences between the shifts and if so, is there one method that gives more benefits. We should consider applying the 4 principles of motion economy, which are:
- Reduce motions
- Perform motions simultaneously
- Reduce distances/effort
- Make motion easier

It may be during our observations that a new method becomes evident which improves the ratio of value added. We must be conscious, however, that we do not introduce unsafe working practices. Consultation with the operators is important to ensure that any new procedure can be followed safely. Finally, once the new method is proved, we can write the SOP.

Writing the SOP

To write the SOP keep in mind the acronym KISS, Keep It Simple Stupid. Initially, there is nothing wrong with handwriting the SOP. If so, write in pen and keep everything clear and concise. Avoid waffling and technical terms; whilst we may be familiar with them, we cannot assume that everyone will be. We can use recognised and agreed abbreviations and sketches or photos are useful: a picture is worth a thousand words. We should not assume prior knowledge of the process. Once the SOP has been prepared, put it to the test. Ask an experienced operator to follow it and then someone new to the process.

Ensure the SOP works and is accurate before typing it up and issuing it. It is essential to add the name of the person preparing it, the date and the issue number, in this case, number 01. Future updates will, therefore, be easier to identify.

Returning to our discussions on achieving process stability, the next goal is to focus on equipment reliability.

EQUIPMENT RELIABILITY

The two commonly used terms when measuring equipment reliability are Mean Time Between Failure (MTBF) and Failure Rate. Failure rate is defined as the number of failures divided by the total time in service. Although a piece of equipment may be available, it does not necessarily follow that it is reliable.

Let us clarify the difference between the two:

Availability is the percentage of time the equipment is in an operable state

Reliability is a measure of how long the item performs its intended function.

As an example, a machine may go down 6 minutes in every hour. This translates to an availability of 91.7%. That may sound pretty impressive. Its reliability, however, measured by MTBF, is less than an hour!

As we know from our discussions on metrics, the things that we measure will improve. The starting point to improve equipment reliability, therefore, is to track these two measures. To improve them, we need to use the seven basic tools of quality, which we discussed earlier. Tracking equipment reliability is a key step in our journey to WCM. A key way of improving equipment reliability is through Total Productive Maintenance (TPM)

TOTAL PRODUCTIVE MAINTENANCE – TPM

What is TPM?

First and foremost, it is a tried and tested way of eliminating waste, saving money and making factories better places to work. As its name suggests, it is a system of maintenance covering the entire life of the equipment and the total human resource associated with it. No longer just the preserve of time-served craftsmen and engineers, it involves everyone in the maintenance of the production process. In doing so, it gives operators the knowledge and confidence to manage their own machines.

TPM is a long-term process which ultimately leads to increased skills, higher efficiency and zero losses. It can be the foundation for improvement for an entire production process. What it is not is simply repairing equipment as quickly and efficiently as possible when it breakdowns. Conversely, its aim is to minimise the chances of equipment ever breaking down, ensuring it runs as effectively as possible and, when it fails, repairing it as quickly and efficiently as possible.

All the activities within an effective maintenance system require close working partnerships between the support functions and the operations team. The old days of us and them, must be forgotten. The attitude that 'engineers fix things and production operators break them again' has no place in TPM. Equally, we must not accept the arguments that:-

"It's running all right at the moment, let's leave it"

"We can't spare the time for planned maintenance"

As a TPM system moves towards maturity, machines will still, inevitably break down. When they do fail, however, we must no longer revert to the "Quick Fix". By all means, we should instigate immediate customer protection, but root-cause investigation and elimination must also be the goal. When dealing with a breakdown, TPM promotes adding planned maintenance in parallel with the breakdown repair, subject to current production requirements of course.

TPM ultimately ensures that equipment is designed with maintainability and reliability as the watchwords.

What is Total Productive Maintenance (TPM)?

The widely accepted pillars of TPM are:
- Improvement Activities (embedded in all TPM key drivers)
- Planned Maintenance
- Autonomous Maintenance
- Education & Training (embedded in all TPM key drivers)
- Maintenance Prevention

All of which are supported by a firm foundation of Continuous Improvement and the systematic elimination of waste.

Benefits of TPM

The goals of TPM are quite simple:

Zero Breakdowns – Zero Accidents – Zero Defects.

The underlining premise of TPM is that it does not accept that machine will inevitably fail. TPM simply reminds us that every time a machine fails, something could have been done to prevent it. As a bonus, implementing TPM ultimately reduces the total life-cycle costs of the equipment.

Since it involves utilising the machine operators in the maintenance process, they gradually become the maintainers of the equipment. Ultimately the maintainers become the improvers. In the process, TPM develops the five senses as well as the technical skills of the operators.

To successfully implement TPM, the philosophy across the whole business should be that, 'failure is not inevitable and something could have been done to prevent it'. It demands an answer to the question,

WHAT WILL STOP IT HAPPENING AGAIN?

TPM helps break down barriers to best practice by removing specialisation. Specialists, such as engineers also benefit. By up-skilling the operators, they are able to focus attention on improving preventative measures and removing waste from the life-cycle of the equipment.

TPM focuses on the 6 big losses that impact Availability, Productivity and Quality.

As we recall from our discussions on OEE, Breakdowns and set-ups reduce the 'Available Time' that operators have to add value during 'Operating Time'. Further stoppages and factors which impact on the most effective use of that operating time are idling, minor stoppages and speed losses, i.e. tool breakages, swarf clearance (<10 minutes) and the effect of equipment not running to optimum speeds. This 'Actual Operating Time' is then finally lessened by the impact of defects (rework) and start-up losses (both in quality and the delays that prevent the equipment achieving optimum running conditions).

Loss Elimination through TPM?

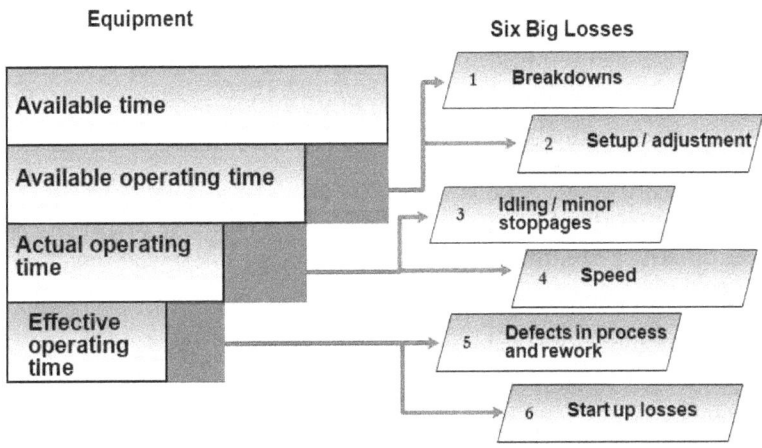

Maintenance Activities

So, practically, if we are to implement TPM, what activities do we need to put in place? It will be no surprise to see some elements already well-embedded in your organisation.

PLANNED MAINTENANCE

This is the scheduling of maintenance activities on a time based or usage basis regardless of the current performance levels of the equipment.

PREVENTATIVE MAINTENANCE

This involves a systematic approach to eliminating catastrophic failure or breakdowns through regular care and attention, early diagnosis and rectification.

PREDICTIVE MAINTENANCE

Here we start to analyse previous failures by using a systematic approach utilising history and equipment condition monitoring to predict and prevent catastrophic failure or breakdowns.

BREAKDOWN MAINTENANCE

When failures occur, instead of simply getting the equipment back into production as soon as possible, we use the breakdown opportunity to our advantage. The goal is to ensure that equipment availability is achieved in the shortest possible time whilst, at the same time, eliminating root cause faults with sustainable repairs.

EFFECTIVE EQUIPMENT DESIGN

A systematic approach to equipment design which maximises equipment availability whilst minimising life-cycle costs and eliminating waste.

AUTONOMOUS MAINTENANCE

This is an operator skills development programme which allows problems to be identified and solved quickly. It is an approach which, when implemented, stops the accelerated deterioration of the plant and equipment and deterioration related failures. It uses what we have already learnt in terms of SOPs through the development of standards. These standards ultimately result in training materials on how to run operate and maintain the equipment.

Autonomous maintenance is the primary way in which production departments can play a part in TPM. Operators are systematically trained in a step-by-step process for cleaning, checking and making minor adjustments to the equipment they work with. In doing so they bring operators and service departments together for a common goal.

Through educating and developing the workforce in autonomous maintenance, we can improve the operation and availability of plant and equipment. This is essential in achieving the first stage of stability required for our lean journey.

As a caveat I should add that introducing autonomous maintenance needs careful thought. There is a saying,

'If you don't train them, don't blame them'

I once went as a consultant into an organisation which, as a cost-saving measure, decided to eliminate the role of quality inspector and have the quality checks carried out by the line operators. The problem was that no one mentioned it to the operators or indeed trained them in their newly required skills! On the day of implementation, as the last QC person was made redundant, chaos reigned as no one fully understood all that the QC people did. Needless to say, the QC role had to be reinstated and the project abandoned.

If we are going to up-skill operators, it is important to involve those currently doing the work. Not to do so will cause resentment and this will frustrate the end goal of implementing autonomous maintenance. How to do so is outside the scope of this book but we will consider this in Book 3 when we discuss Leading4Lean.

MODULE 5

WORKSHOP ORGANISATION

Workshop organisation is a key element of creating the stability we need if we are to achieve a truly lean enterprise. The three elements we are to consider are 5S, equipment layout, and visual factory. All three terms need some explanation, so let us begin with visual factory.

VISUAL FACTORY

Visual factory or visual management is the term used to represent a combination of signs, charts and other visual representation of information that enables the quick dissemination of data in a lean manufacturing process. It allows quick communication of information about the equipment's current operating conditions and environment through the use of Visual Aids.

It points out what is correct and identifies what has changed. This results in the quick identification of problems. It identifies when equipment is operating correctly and when not, instigating early treatment prior to failure.

What Visual Management is not is a way to make a plant look 'pretty'; unfortunately, this is often how senior management views it. I remember an incident during a particular lean implementation when we were still in the developing solutions phase. A director of the company who was also the project sponsor was frustrated by what appeared to him to be the slow progress of the project. Having heard why we were not yet ready for the implementation stage, he said, "Well, at least put a load of signs around the place, you know, visual management and all!"

Clearly, this is not the point. Visual Management is there to provide information relevant to the smooth operation of the area. It involves everyone in the operation in the process of managing improvement. To be effective it must be used every day. If once installed but the visual aids are not being used - TAKE THEM DOWN! There is nothing worse than progress graphs for example, prominently displayed which, when examined, show the information to be three months out of date!

Here is a little test for your operation. In 5 seconds, does a stranger visiting your section know what's going on? Is he or she able to 'see the factory', its workflow, its performance, its problems and its opportunities for improvements. If not, you are not yet there with the aims of visual management, also known as visual factory.

Empowerment, the key to Employee Involvement in WCM, is not possible without information, and the best way to ensure that information is available is through simple visual aids. Information about production activities, processes, and the results against agreed targets should be displayed visually and clearly so that they are self-apparent and obvious to all. Information above all should be transparent. The number of defects and waste should be so blatantly obvious, that it is impossible to ignore them. Visual display of information should ultimately lead to visual control.

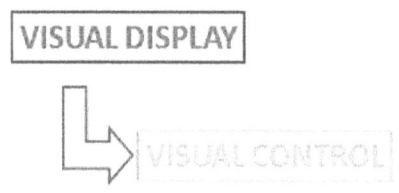

So what kind of information relevant to the process should we be displaying? Types of Visual Display might include:
- Hourly production against target
- Flashing lights to show faults in the process including stoppage.
- Quality data, scrap, etc.
- Skills Matrix for members of the production team.
- A graph showing absenteeism levels.

If an abnormal condition is identified in the visual display, this should lead to an action.

Examples of Visual Control which lead to an action are:
- Red flashing light on the machine.
- Pull System signal (KANBAN).
- SPC charts, control limits reached.
- Poor quality part produced.
- Hourly output not achieved.

A 'Nervous System' for the Operation

We discussed at the start of this book the differences between traditional manufacturing operations and lean operations. In the former, data is gathered on the shop floor and is then manipulated by several people before being reported back to the shop floor, often several days later. Any chance to rectify a problem is lost in the time delay between collecting the data and reporting it.

Visual Factory offers a way of creating a "NERVOUS SYSTEM." In this case, we record data as a Visual Display so that we can react immediately when abnormal conditions occur. So, how do we achieve Visual Control?

Achieving Visual Control

The first step is to identify the key information we need to monitor the operation. We have already discussed KPIs so we know to focus on parameters that have a direct impact on our success which, if improved, will improve both profitability and productivity. There is a story about a Russian nail factory continually missing its targets in the five-year plan, in this case failing to produce its quota of 5,000 tonnes of nails per year. A new director was sort who easily met the target in his first year – he had the factory produce one, 5,000-tonne nail! In hindsight, maybe his target should have been the number of nails per year (and thus per hour) rather than the weight!

To achieve Visual Control, we must:

- Visually Display the Information
- Define who and how often to update the display.
- Define the normal and abnormal conditions.
- Define how to highlight the abnormal conditions.
- Define an action that will bring the Operation back into the Normal Condition.

Examples of Production Output Monitors

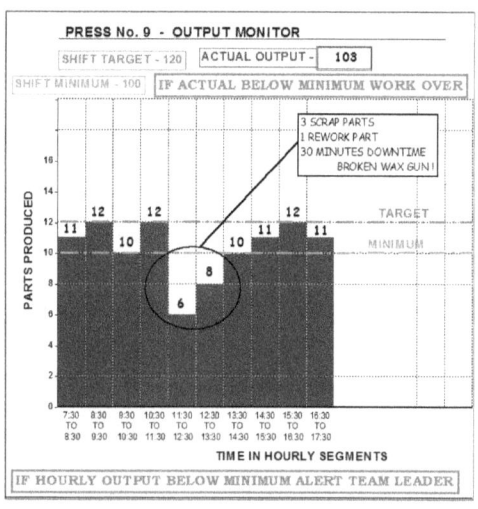

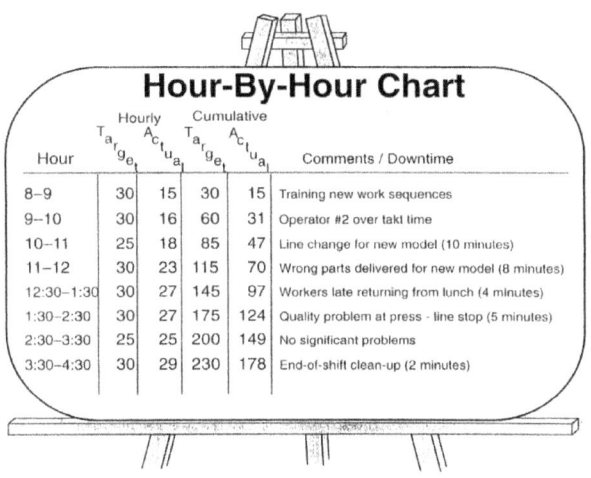

Hour-By-Hour Chart

Hour	Hourly Target	Actual	Cumulative Target	Actual	Comments / Downtime
8–9	30	15	30	15	Training new work sequences
9–10	30	16	60	31	Operator #2 over takt time
10–11	25	18	85	47	Line change for new model (10 minutes)
11–12	30	23	115	70	Wrong parts delivered for new model (8 minutes)
12:30–1:30	30	27	145	97	Workers late returning from lunch (4 minutes)
1:30–2:30	30	27	175	124	Quality problem at press - line stop (5 minutes)
2:30–3:30	25	25	200	149	No significant problems
3:30–4:30	30	29	230	178	End-of-shift clean-up (2 minutes)

An example of a Skills Matrix:

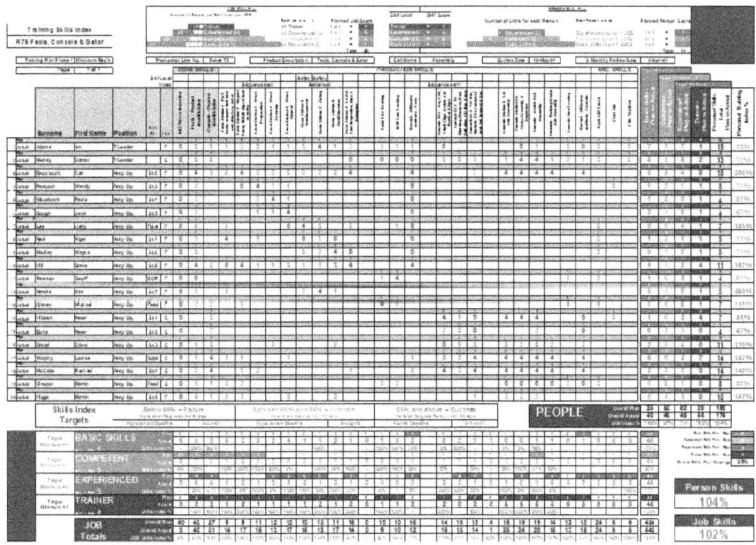

Notice how a traffic light system is used to highlight when a target has been achieved by marking it with green. When working towards a target amber is used and when there is a non-conformance and work is required, red.

A particularly useful form of visual factory is known as Andon Lights which builds on this idea.

ANDON SYSTEM

In traditional companies, the chain of command comes from the top and goes straight down. Lean operates with a different approach in that it is the process itself that initiates actions. One method is the use of Andon, a lean technique that empowers the operator to highlight abnormalities in the process and obtain support from above to continue to meet the plan.

An Andon system forms an important business measure of the health of a production line. It could be considered similar to the nervous system in our own bodies. By highlighting the concern in a timely fashion it maximises the chance of solving the problem before it affects productivity.

Andon helps support the principle of an inverse management pyramid where, instead of the workers being there to support the management and follow their instructions and requests, management is there to support workers and provide them with the help they need to resolve issues.

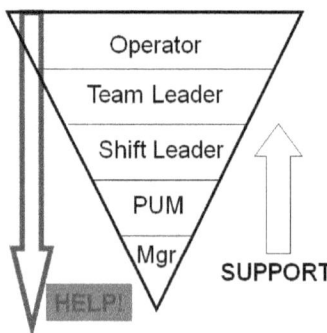

It is an information tool which provides an instant, visible and audible warning to the operations team that there is an abnormality within that area.

The key words are:
INSTANT
VISIBLE and AUDIBLE
WARNING

Andon on it's on its own does not actually achieve anything. To fulfil its purpose, it needs a timely RESPONSE to make the Andon system effective.

Different forms of Andon

An Andon can take many different forms from simple indicator to complex control boards. All of them give 'real time' status of the performance of the given area. Andon systems come in all shapes and sizes, dependent on the requirement. In its simplest form, it could be an airport security check, the petrol gauge indicator in our car or even the low battery indicator on our mobile.

Standard line side systems often use the lollipop or traffic light system we mentioned earlier. (RED/AMBER/GREEN) More complex systems often use Andon boards which in some cases may be a VDU. Complex Andon systems can highlight every type of abnormality and where it originated, for example in a chemical plant, while others just draw attention to a concern that needs to be addressed. The system ultimately will be dependent on the budget available and the complexity of the workplace. We look at different types of Andon systems later in the module.

So, what exactly does an Andon system do? Andon allows timely corrective actions by alerting personnel when abnormal conditions occur. It allows shop-floor team leaders to spend less time and effort monitoring the situation, and more time-solving abnormalities. It allows operation teams to monitor equipment and personnel more effectively. It can act as a 2-way communication device e.g. when indicator returns to green; this tells everybody it's 'back to normal.'

It is very important to understand what an Andon system is capable of. It has its limitations. It should not be seen as a panacea for all production abnormalities. To summarise, Andon **will** highlight concerns and abnormalities. It will provide information to allow the management of concerns. What it **will** **not** do is solve abnormalities. Without a robust escalation procedure and corrective action process, it is worthless.

What an Andon system also does not do is prevent all defects from being passed forward. However effective, it cannot replace good verbal communication between members of the workgroup. It does not remove the need for rectification or customer protection either, in fact, IT DOESN'T SOLVE ANYTHING. If you are considering putting in an Andon system, it is important to make sure that everybody understands that it is not an excuse for not doing anything.

Installing an Andon system may mean that rework has to be done or some level of containment is put in place.

Andon should not replace human interaction within the workgroup. Whilst good communication practices are enhanced by the use of Andon, it still requires that problems are solved as soon as possible.

The Natural Workgroup

Andon can only be effective if the team leader is backed up by an issue resolution procedure.

As mentioned earlier, the abnormality still needs to be addressed if it is not to affect the performance of that work area. This is done by identifying the 'natural workgroup' that interfaces with that work area. It is important that individuals are identified and are accessible to the workgroup. This means giving all operators the NAMES and NUMBERS of the members of the group.

Once an issue is raised, then the 'natural workgroup' must support that request as soon as possible. If the issue isn't eliminated in a timely fashion then the system should escalate to the next appropriate level. By doing so, the abnormality will eventually be addressed and a long-term countermeasure put in place to prevent future occurrence.

For example, earlier we referred to Airport security. If nothing happened when the alarm went off, it would be worthless. Ironically, whenever a car alarm goes off, instead of spurring people in the vicinity to action, most people will ignore it and more likely curse the car owner for disturbing them!

An example of a Natural Workgroup:

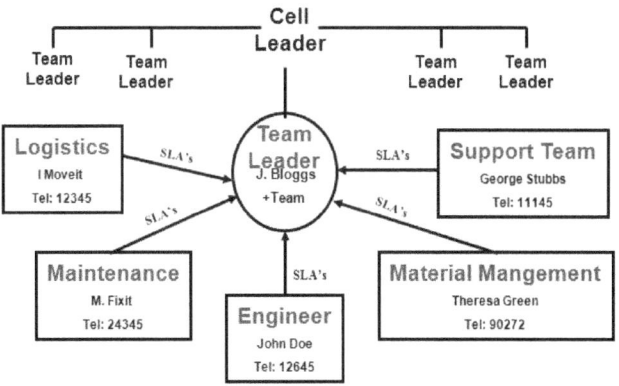

Features of an Andon system

When installing an Andon system, the key elements to consider are:

Visible/Audible – It should be positioned where it can be seen and/or heard by the entire workgroup and workgroup leader. In one operation I managed, an injection moulding shop, the Andon board was suspended over the banks of machines and was visible from both sides. When a machine cycled its position on the board flashed. When it stopped completely, its light stayed on prompting the machine setter to action. It was affectionately known as the 'Bingo Board'

Concise/Understandable – It is important to keep it simple. An Andon system should cover three primary conditions. When the process is OK, where there is an abnormality and when the process has stopped. In the case of the Bingo Board, OK was signified by the light flashing as the machine cycled. When there was an abnormality, such as a moulding bridging the machine, stopping it recycling, the light stayed on. When the machine was considered to be stopped, defined by a timer set to two minutes, a second red light came on, signifying that the operator needed to be in attendance.

Timely/Responsive – The Andon MUST operate with real-time data. Unless it reflects the actual situation, it is no better than a written report after the event. For cycling machinery, a sensor on a particular stage of the cycle is often used to gather data.

Pertinent – It should only show the status of workstations in a particular area over which the operator(s) has control.

Complete – It must provide a complete picture of the overall status of the entire area to enable prioritisation and coordination of corrective efforts. Without these features, the Andon system will have limited beneficial use. If they are followed, however, then the Andon system will be of great help in eliminating abnormalities in the workplace

Types of Andon system

There are two main types of Andon systems, manual and automatic. A manual system is activated by the operator, team leader or both. This may involve pressing a static button or pulling a cord. Cords are often used on a moving line. This allows the operator to raise the alarm at any time during their work cycle. This system is used where the operator is unable to move far from the product. This can be for safety reasons or usually due to very tight work cycle time. Again this system can be used by multiple operators and is usually placed above the head of the operator.

It can be used by the operator to gain assistance to highlight either production or maintenance concerns. If it is an assembly line, on activation, the line will stop at a predetermined position. This ensures the line does not stop when somebody is working on the line.

Automatic Andon systems include automatic sensors, automatic trips, light guards and fixed position stop. Examples of automatic Andon systems are:

- The weight of a box of parts holds down the limit switch until it is taken and the switch activates the Andon to highlight that the last box has gone.

- A simple light beam across the front of a box will trigger the switch if it is not broken in the right order (i.e. the operator is assembling the product away from standard)

- A limit switch on a conveyor or on a chute monitoring the movement of parts.

Andon systems can be as complex as the business dictates. For example, in the car industry, electronic systems can cost millions of pounds and display vast amounts of information.

Escalation Process

When the Andon system signals an alert, an escalation procedure needs to be in place to guide the operator. In the car industry, stoppages and the subsequent loss of production are very expensive and must be avoided at all costs. The escalation procedure is designed to engage the correct resource and decision makers at every stage.

Stage 1

Once an abnormality is identified it is escalated to the next level to eliminate it. This could be a more senior operator. If the next level cannot eliminate it, however, then it is raised to the Shift Leader.

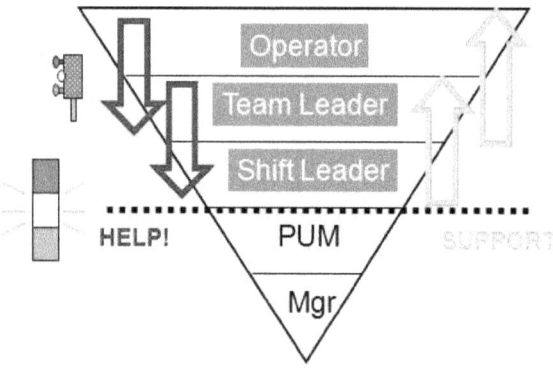

Stage 2

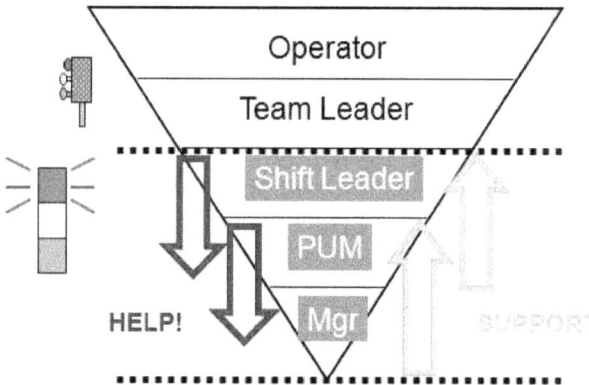

Once all efforts to solve the problem have been exhausted at Shift Leader level, the problem is escalated to the highest level to avoid the line stopping.

SETTING UP AN ANDON SYSTEM

WHO: This should be done by the operations team.

WHAT: The operations team must determine what production conditions need to be monitored, what needs to be controlled and what Andon system meets their needs and is appropriate for the workplace.

Andon signals should be simple and easy to understand. The temptation is to spend too much money on a 'State of the Art' Andon System. Before investing in such a system, the best way is to prove it with a simple manual system in order to judge its worth. It is important that the Andon system is visible and audible from every corner of the work relevant work area.

WHERE: The operation should be divided into several processes or stations and assign each a process number or code and, as important, an owner. Usually, a small team is assigned to each process number or code. The process numbers or codes are posted at the line side stations where they are easily visible.

WHY: To enable the operations team to expose abnormalities with their process so as to help eliminate them.

WHEN: The Andon system should only be installed after a robust escalation procedure has been implemented. Each operator and support members must be fully aware of their role in the escalation procedure before the system is made live.

HOW: The characteristics of the production line should be documented together with data history for the line. Next, the Andon procedures should be tied together with the audit procedures.

Once the Andon system is in use, its benefits stretch well beyond the smooth running of the process. Rather than just responding to effects, it's use is fundamental in highlighting abnormalities and then eliminating them.

By analysing data and the frequency of Andon pulls by the operator, the workgroups can identify and focus on improving abnormality and bottleneck areas. Andon systems are like all systems, they are only as good as the people who design them and use them. If they are strictly adhered to and designed appropriately, then they will drastically improve the performance of the process. However, they are not the panacea to all problems, and should not be viewed as such.

Once established, the response times from the support functions and Andon pulls should be closely monitored. Constructive use of Andon systems can build up data, which can be used to permanently eliminate the abnormalities which torment everybody in the workplace. These simple systems can be the starting point for the serious productivity and profitability improvements needed to become a truly lean enterprise and ultimately a World Class Manufacturer.

One final reminder; Andon systems do not solve abnormalities; they only highlight them in time to rectify the situation quickly.

MODULE 6

THE FIVE PILLARS – 5S

Commonly known as the five pillars of the visual workplace, 5S stands for:

Sort, Set-in-Order, Shine, Standardise and Sustain.

Although a great play is made of the fact that the words are a translation from the Japanese, the principles involved are probably as old as time itself. As I said earlier, 5S follows the logic of having 'a place for everything and everything in its place.' Let us start by defining 5S as:

A tool that creates a work environment that is disciplined and in which it is easy to tell if an abnormality is occurring so that it can be resolved.

5S is the organized, relentless, never-ending effort to remove all physical waste out of the workplace, set things in order, inspect it constantly, and have a culture that promotes, endorses and rewards all of the above, from management to the shop floor. It is a key element of Visual Factory. So, what are the benefits of implementing 5S?

Benefits to you as an employee
- Gives you an input on how your workplace should be organized
- Makes your workplace better to work in
- Makes your job more satisfying
- Removes obstacles and frustrations
- Helps you know what is expected of you
- Makes communication easier

Benefits to the company
- Helps reduce changeover times by having an orderly workplace
- Helps reduce defects by Sort and Set in Order

- Helps reduce waste (e.g. the time spent searching for components)
- Improves deliveries by reducing delays
- Improves Health and Safety
- Cleaning equipment and the workplace helps reduce breakdowns
- Reduces defects and delays and improves Customer Service Level (CSL)
- Improved CSL leads to Corporate growth

Let us look at each element of 5S in detail:

THE FIRST PILLAR - SORT

SORT means that we remove all items from the workplace that are not needed for the current production. At first, it may be difficult to distinguish between what is needed and what is not. For example, unneeded inventory, equipment or quality defects should not be in the workplace. This is 'prime real estate' and should be guarded jealously and not contaminated with clutter. The starting point is to conduct an initial audit. Implementation of 5S is fundamentally a team effort and should be approached as such although delegation of areas to individuals is also part of this process. Once the initial audit is complete, the team is now ready to begin the 5S process. Sorting is also known in the alternative method known as the 5C's as 'clear out and classify' and is the process of determining what is required and what is not.

During the initial audit, tags are used to identify all the equipment in the area that operators do not use as part of their day-to-day work. Once all the work area has been covered, all tagged items should be removed to a quarantine area. These items are then held pending action after the next stage, **SET IN ORDER.**

During the **SORT** stage, the team will need to create storage or holding points for equipment that has been identified. One of the points will be for **KEEP** and the other for **QUARANTINE**. When publicising this exercise, a useful way of categorising items is by considering the slogan, 'Use it or lose it!' As mentioned earlier, the immediate workplace area is 'prime real estate'. Every item inspected, therefore, needs to justify it right to occupy this area.

The disposal action will be determined by the frequency of use of an item or by its relative importance to the area. High frequency of use items i.e. hourly/daily should be kept on the operator, possibly on a work belt or stored in the correct orientation at the workplace. Items which are used weekly/quarterly should be stored at a location that is near to the workplace but not in it, preferably at a central location within the factory.

Items that are used infrequently i.e. twice a year or less should be investigated to try and eliminate the need for them completely. One option is to combine its use with something else or, failing this, it should be stored away and archived somewhere appropriate where it can be retrieved in a speedy manner. (Dumping it behind the factory, under tarpaulin is often seen to be the solution until it is needed and then, nine times out of ten the item is no longer usable).

In summary, when considering items stored in the workplace:

Classify tooling / equipment by frequency of use

Code	Description	Action
HIGH	Hourly	Keep at workplace
MEDIUM	Daily/Weekly	Store at dept store
LOW	Quarterly/6 Monthly	Store away from area or dispose

.......within the LOW category, retrieval MUST still be quick!!

Red-Tag Strategy

This is an effective use of visual factory which we discussed earlier. It involves putting red tags on any items not required for the current production, any items kept in excessive amounts and any items used infrequently. Once an item has a red-tag attached, it should be removed from the area/cell.

A Red Tag Exercise is conducted to essentially remove all the unnecessary items (tool, chairs, tables, paperwork etc.) from the area being assessed. A structured process must be followed if success is to be realised, the following diagram shows a structured approach which must be undertaken.

110

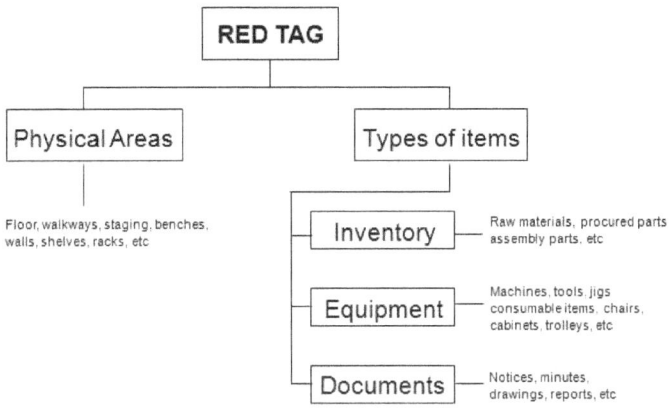

......Red Tag Targets

The first red tag exercise is best undertaken with a facilitator who has previous experience. The facilitator must explain to the team what items can be red tagged. If this process is not followed, items that are currently used for production may be accidentally removed from the area. Every effort must be made ensure needed items are not removed.

The diagram above gives numerous examples of items the team is likely to come across which may be red tagged and ultimately removed from the area/cell.

Red Tag Auctions

As you might expect, different team members will have different views on the merits of an item remaining in the work area. To ensure the team all agree on the items that are to be removed, it is recommended that the facilitator conducts a Red Tag Auction.

This auction should take place in the area where the items have been quarantined and should involve all of the key decision makers (to ensure a decision can be immediately made on whether to dispose of an item or not). The options to consider are:

- Keep the item where it is.
- Move it to a new location in work area.
- Store away from the work area.
- Hold in Red Tag Quarantine Area for evaluation at a later stage.
- Dispose of the item. This might include throwing it away immediately or simply returning it to stores.

During the process, the team should agree on the minimum and maximum quantities allowable for each item.

Record the Results

Records need to be kept of the items moved to a Red Tagging Area or disposed of. The team should briefly cover off every item that's been red-tagged and use the options above to decide what to do with each tagged item.

It is recommended that the team capture all actions on red tagged items for future analysis using a 'RED TAG ANALYSIS SHEET,' an example of which is shown below.

Red Tag Analysis Sheet

NO.	ITEM	VALUE(£)	REQUIRED YES	NO	ACTION	WHO	WHEN

Note : Value Categories are   £ 0-100   /   £100-1000   /   £1000+

Why Sort?

The merits of SORT might seem blindingly obvious but, trust me, I have been in many production operations where it is ignored. The problem with accepting clutter is that people will feel licensed to add to it. As a consultant, I used to ask clients 'if they had a magic wand, what would they wish for?' One of the most common answers was 'more space.' My response was that they actually had more than enough space already; they were simply using it badly. I am not suggesting SORT on its own is the panacea for gaining more space. We will consider this in more detail when we discuss workplace layout and eventually Value Stream Mapping in Book 3. It is, however, a key tool in the lean toolbox for releasing space in an existing layout. Let us summarise the advantages of conducting a SORT exercise:

- It frees up space.
- It removes clutter and obstacles from the workplace
- It stops people adding to it.
- It stops people hoarding unnecessary items in the workplace.
- It improves safety.
- It introduces control of what is allowed in the work area.
- It begins the 'orderliness' process which we will consider next.

THE SECOND PILLAR – SET IN ORDER

SET in ORDER is the logical outcome of the SORT exercise. Once the items that need to remain in the work area have been agreed, the next step is to arrange these in a way that means they are easy to use and easy to find and put away.

For example, where tools and jigs are needed in the work area, a storage board can be added. If for example, we need screwdrivers, these can be numbered and allocated individual places on the storage board. Often their outline is painted in black beneath. This is often called a shadow board. In this way, if tools are missing it is immediately evident. Also, if the wrong tool is returned to that location, it is equally obvious.

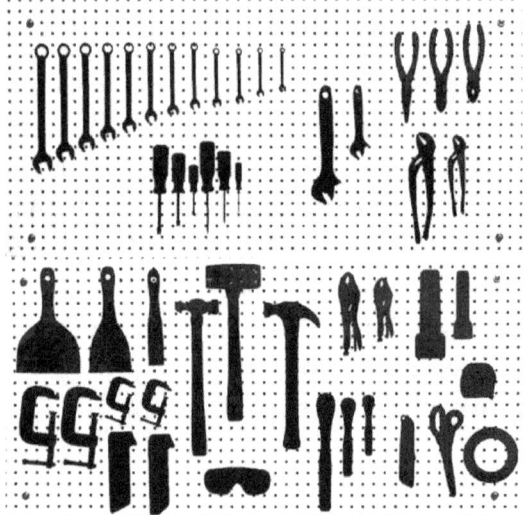

Another advantage of Setting in Order is that it gives us the opportunity to arrange all necessary items for economy of movement. The place closest to the workplace should be assigned by assessing the frequency of use of the items; the most used being closest to the point of use.

The purpose of Set in Order is to have a designated place for everything. This allows us to label it, classify it and make it easily visible for other users.

Setting in Order allows us to provide safe storage. If racking is used, then the heavy items can be stored on the lowest levels, or even the floor, and the lighter items on higher racking.

Later in the programme we will be discussing in detail the idea of 'flow', a key elemental of a lean operation. Setting in Order allows items to be placed in such a manner as to assist flow. Everything in the workplace should have an appointed 'home,' the place where it lives and can be easily found. Again we

114

need to think about those items which are used most frequently and stored for regular use. Those items and materials which are regarded as being relevant to daily operation will determine the optimum place to keep them and the orientation in which they should be stored. We can summarise Set in Order with this simple phrase:

A PLACE FOR EVERYTHING AND EVERYTHING IN ITS PLACE.

Examples of Set in Order:

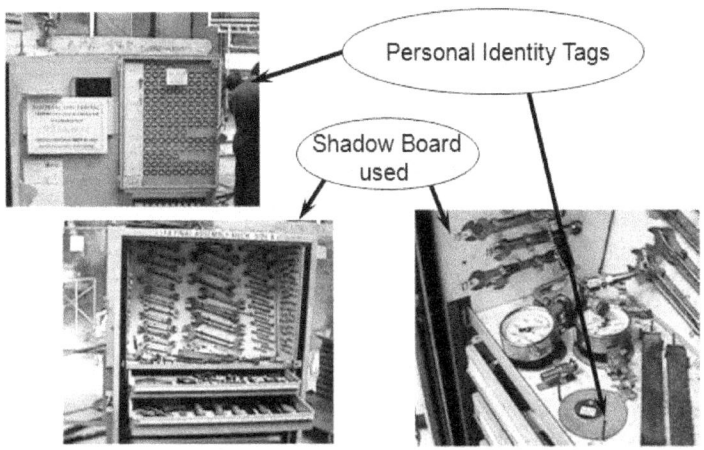

The above diagram illustrates examples of Set in Order. It shows how the issue of tools can be controlled using Personal Identity Tags shown at the top left corner of the diagram. The operator takes a tool from the storage cabinet and places his or her personalised tag in the on. This assists when another operator needs to use the same tool. It is immediately evident who is currently using it.

At the bottom left of the diagram, it shows the wide variety of tools that are shadowed within the storage cabinet. The bottom right of the diagram shows how the tag is located when an operator takes a tool.

Why Set in Order?

Set in order makes things easier to find, use and return. This, in turn, removes the frustration of searching for items. As important, it creates a better working environment, reduces accidents and assists cleanliness. It also starts the process of STANDARDISATION, the fourth pillar of 5S

THE THIRD PILLAR – SHINE

SHINE means sweeping floors, wiping down machinery and generally making sure that everything in the factory stays clean. **SHINE** is closely related to the ability to turn out quality products. It also includes saving labour by finding ways to prevent dirt, dust, and debris from piling up in the workplace.

To introduce SHINE, the first step is to identify cleaning zones across the workplace. The workplace is subdivided into areas of individual responsibility and the names of these individuals are displayed. In this way, everyone becomes accountable for keeping the workplace clean. In my forty plus years in manufacturing, ensuring that operators kept the work area clean and tidy was always one of my biggest bug-bears. Somehow, when challenged, it seemed that the mess was always created by someone else, the other shift, another operator or perhaps a wayward tooth fairy passing through. By nominating responsibility for an area to named individuals, it cuts through all the excuses and is one of the simplest ways of bottoming the problem.

Once the areas and people responsible are identified, they are given targets which they must work to. Instead of the usual mad clean up prior to a major customer or senior management visit, employees must keep their area clean and tidy on a continual basis.

Cleanliness also extends to non-seen areas. For example, the area under the jig, behind the cupboards and even on top of the cupboards should be monitored. Routine maintenance which we discussed under TPM may be incorporated into the cleaning schedules.

SHINE (or Clean and Check under 5C) is not just a one-off event but it is a continual process. A five-minute daily sweep will prevent the need to 'Blitz' the work area. In the 5S programme, this step also introduces the concept of solving problems in the work area, particularly machine or equipment related problems. It is worth remembering the saying; 'through cleaning you touch, through touching you find faults thereby fixing them'. We should use SHINE to inspect equipment and find abnormalities early. If you are the team leader of the area, this is the opportunity to promote visual standards and get the team to buy into them.

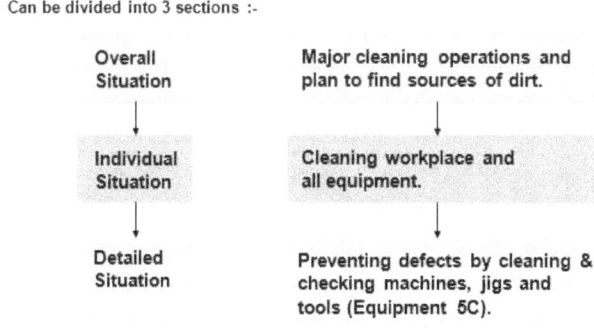

SHINE can be divided into three areas as shown in the above diagram.

Overall situation

Here we consider what the overall strategy will look like for the area as a whole. What we do not do is get bogged down in detailed cleaning activities.

Individual situation

This step is more focused on the operator's immediate area and what he or she needs to do, and when to maintain an agreed standard of cleanliness. This activity needs to be enforced in the early stages to ensure the process is maintained.

Detailed situation

This is more focused on the maintenance of individual items of equipment. For example, if a tool is used it is the responsibility of the machine operator to ensure it is adequately cleaned after use and all necessary pins are attached to the tool before being returned to a storage area.

SHINE and Total Productive Maintenance.

The introduction of 5S and the discipline of making the operator responsible for cleaning their machine and work area is a perfect opportunity to begin the process of TPM. The starting point is to introduce a cleaning check sheet, an example of which is shown below:

Machine: M/c 1265		Date: 15/08		Completed by: J Brown			
No	**Location / Fault**	**Code class**	**Cause**	**Temp Perm**	**Countermeasure**	**Who**	**When**
1	Pressure Gauge not within limit	H3	Poor labelling	T	Ensure manual setting on label	Team	1/11
				P	Write Setting on Setting sheet	Team	1/11
2	Measuring probe unprotected next to pallet	E9	Poor design	T	Cover to be made	NCMT	Wk 26
				P	Review machine specification	MR	Wk 26
3	Oil Leak next to twin pallet	L4	Poorly installed	T	Fix leak	Maint	Wk 25
				P	Review installation procedure	MR	Wk 27

Code	E		M		L		H		P		W
	Electrical		Mechanical		Lubrication		Hydraulic		Pneumatic		Water
Class	1	2	3	4	5	6	7	8		9	
	Loose	Worn	Broken	Leaking	Missing	Dirty	Difficult to clean	Location / Routing		Poor design	

The information collected can be used to conduct a fault analysis. The following chart shows how this might be analysed:

CONCERN / FAULT ANALYSIS

	E	M	L	H	W	P	TOTAL
1							
2							
3							
4							
5							
6							
7							
8							
9							
TOTAL							

CODE CLASS

E = ELECTRICAL
M = MECHANICAL
L = LUBRICATION
H = HYDRAULIC
W = WATER
P = PNEUMATIC

1 = LOOSE
2 = WORN
3 = BROKEN
4 = LEAKING
5 = MISSING
6 = DIRTY
7 = DIFFICULT TO CLEAN
8 = LOCATION & / OR ROUTING

9 = POOR DESIGN

Why Shine?

Shine (or Clean and Check) makes defects easier to detect. It is almost impossible to promote high levels of product quality in a dirty or untidy area. It has the further advantage of improving customer perception. If it looks right, it usually is! Shine creates a better working environment and aids efficiency and reduces accidents. The introduction of SHINE is an essential step in STANDARDIZATION.

THE FOURTH PILLAR – STANDARDIZE

Once we have prepared the workplace, the next important element is to maintain it through standardization. **STANDARDIZE** differs from the first three which can be thought of as activities. We can define STANDARDIZE as the result that exists when we maintain the first three pillars - SORT, SET in ORDER, and SHINE.

The key goals of STANDARDIZE are:
- To promote the use of visual controls.
- To maintain the workplace at a level which uncovers and makes problems obvious.
- To continuously improve by continuous assessment and generating actions.
- To include routine Health and Safety in our checks.
- To ensure that the system is controlled and maintained (using agreed standards.)
- To have a standard operating procedure to ensure that the first three parts of 5S are not done once and then forgotten.
- To establish and agree on standards that everyone works to - e.g. documentation, filing systems, best practices.
- To make the standard such that any newcomer can join the section and quickly work to the set standard.

Over time the adherence to this new standard will become **custom and practice**. One important way of ensuring this is to implement 5S audits as part of the STANDARDIZE process. These can be done individually, for example as part of a shift handover or as an impromptu or periodic inspection by members of the team working together. The areas for inspection are set down on a 5S Audit Check Sheet. The advantages of using a check sheet are:
- It promotes continual assessment.
- It helps maintain the set standard.
- It enables a Plan, Do, Check, Action cycle.
- It promotes safety first.
- It allows publishing the scores on company notice boards.
- It impresses the customer.

When auditing, it is important that the team apply common sense. The audit allows the team to clearly see whether a standard is being worked to or not. If the answer is no, then the team needs to take action and ask the question WHY???

It may be that the standard is inappropriate. In this case, the team must collectively agree to develop an appropriate standard in a timely manner.

If the standard is found to be appropriate then the team must be re-trained to ensure effective implementation.

As mentioned earlier, one valuable use of a 5S audit sheet is for handovers, where jobs are shared between a number of people, usually on shift working.

Self-Audit/Handover Sheet

An example of a self-audit sheet is shown below:

ITEMS	INDIVIDUAL INSTANCES IN WORKPLACE AREA AUDITED	TOTAL No. OF INSTANCES	SCORE	POINTS
Dirt & rubbish on floor (paper/pkgs, dunnage etc.)			0 = No Dirt/Rubbish 5 = 1 - 5 Instances 10 = >5 Instances	0 5 10
Oil grease or other spillages where Machine is dirty and neglected.			0 = All machines clean 10 = 1 - 5 Machines 15 = >5 Machines	0 10 15
Locations of materials not defined. Mixed access materials in store.			0 = All locations defined 10 = 1 - 5 Instances 15 = >5 Instances	0 10 15
Notice boards untidy & out of date. No ref to OCD.			0 = OCD Up to-Date 5 = <50% Incorrect 10 = >50% Incorrect	0 5 10
Safety equipm and procedures not adhered to.			0 = Safe operation 15 = Some procedures not used	0 15
Lights left switched on & lighting, energy wasted.			0 = No Instances 5 = <3 Instances 10 = >3 Instances	0 5 10
Unnecessary materials & equipment in work area			0 = All necessary 3 = 1 - 5 instances 10 = >5 Instances	0 5 10
Reject parts not clearly identified or segregated.			0 = All clearly identified / segregated 15 = Not all identified	0 15
COMMENTS		TOTAL	IMPROVEMENT POTENTIAL	

The first step in the process requires that the team leader together with his or her team take responsibility for their work areas. It may sound simple but in my experience, when areas are shared with others there is always an excuse for poor housekeeping. It inevitably follows one of Homer Simpson's 3-

step rules for success at work - 'it was broke when I got here!' (The other two are, 'that's a good idea, boss' and 'cover for me!')

This sheet can be part of a team leader's hand-over log and should be agreed by both outgoing and incoming team leaders, preferably with a face to face meeting. The question they must agree on is - does this reflect the state of the work area? The areas they should be considering are:

- Is the housekeeping to the required standard?
- Are performance management measures up to date and on target?
- Are quality standards adhered to?
- Is work is being performed to the standard?
- Are issues identified and customer protection or countermeasures underway?

As well as handover and self-assessment audits, most companies often institute a weekly management audit of the department. The stats of 5S should be one of the key KPIs for the department and as such should be reviewed regularly. As with all KPIs, targets should be set and trends monitored. The results should be displayed openly in the section. It is important that the results are fed back to those responsible for the area to ensure that remedial actions for non-compliances can be promptly taken. An example of a management audit is shown below:

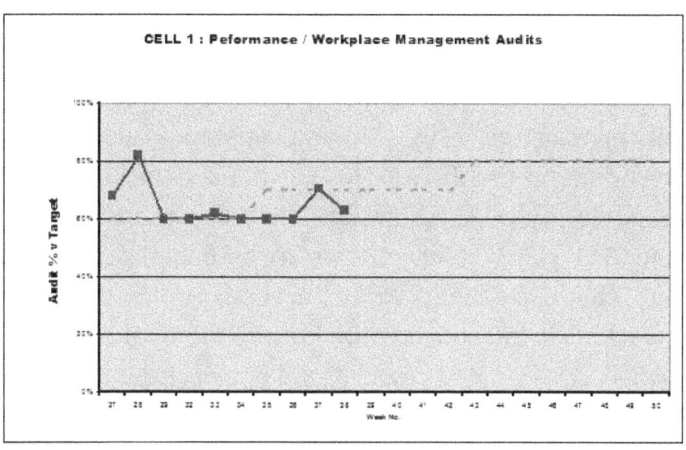

CELL 1 : Peformance / Workplace Management Audits

The information from the audits is then a key measure for improving the workplace and its performance.

Housekeeping Area Map

As we discussed earlier, team leaders and members should be made responsible for their work areas. The way to achieve this is to prepare a housekeeping area map with the names of each team member across all shifts identified. The area for the team leader should be clearly marked on this map. I have often seen the names displayed in the area itself as well as on the housekeeping map.

Why STANDARDIZE?

In summary, STANDARDIZE provides a schedule of 5S activities. It ensures deterioration of the first three pillars does not occur. It provides a standard for all team members to work to and starts problem solving/improvement activities. By continually auditing the workplace it makes the first 3S's a habit. Most importantly, it promotes ownership. By involving the workforce in writing and defining the standards it helps to ensure they will buy into and follow them.

123

THE FIFTH PILLAR – SUSTAIN

Perhaps the most difficult of the five pillars, **SUSTAIN** means making a habit of properly maintaining correct procedures. The four pillars can be only be implemented successfully if employees commit to SUSTAINING 5S. In many factories, a lot of effort is made in SORTING and SHINING because they lack the discipline to SUSTAIN. I am sure we are all familiar with 'flavour of the month' management where, in a flurry of activity, a new way of working is introduced only for it to fall by the wayside as the normal day-to-day pressures take priority. This is not unusual, it is everyone's problem. In Leading4Lean in Book 3, I explain a formula we can use, as managers, supervisors and team leaders to help in sustaining not just 5S but any new ideas introduced to the team. If you wish to know more detail now, I suggest you read my book, Leadership – a Formula for Success.

The key to SUSTAIN is to make 5S a habit. We need to practice and report until it becomes a way of life. One way of achieving this is to set up a review frequency using visual communication rather than verbal.

A good example, often seen in restrooms in supermarkets and eating places such as McDonald's, is a cleaning checklist matrix. Its purpose is to visually assure the customer that the restroom has been inspected by a member of the staff at a regular frequency. There are no ifs or buts; the signature confirms the 5S STANDARDIZE procedure is being followed. Its key to success is that it promotes **Ownership!** The person(s) named on the housekeeping map are held accountable for the inspection together with the remedial action required if the restroom is not to standard. A similar example, an operator checklist in a manufacturing operation is shown below:

124

Machine: Gieason		Process: Gear Cutting		Date: November																	

Cleaning Item	Std / Lub	Time (min)	1 T		2 W		3 TH		4 F		7 M		8 T		9 W		10 TH		11 F		14 M		15 T		16 W		17 TH		18 F		2 M
			1	2	1	2	1	2	1	2	1	2	1	2	1	2	1	2	1	2	1	2	1	2	1	2	1	2	1	2	1
Hydraulic Tank	Clean	2	√	√	√	√																										
Machine body	No swarf	3	√	√	√	√																										
Machine body	Clean	1	√	√	√	√																										
Machine base	Clean	4	√		√																											
Liquid lines	Clean	1	√																													
Motor Fan	Clean	1	√																													
Lubrication Standard																															
Pump	No excess	1	√	√	√	√																										
Spindles	No excess	1	√		√																											
Lubricator	GP Oil	1	√	√	√	√																										
Filter	No water	2	√		√																											
Regulator	To limits	1	√		√																											
Lubricator	To limits	1	√		√																											
Check Press Gauge	In limits	1	√	√	√	√																										
Check Temp Gauge	In limits	1	√	√	√	√																										
Check Main Spindle	No play	2	√	√	√	√																										

The results of these checks can be put on visual display as a graph to show improvement trends or to identify where there are problems to enable problem-solving to take place. Using this audit style ensures that 5S standards become CUSTOM and PRACTICE

The 5S process is a waste of time if we do not have the self-discipline to capture the improvements that the team has made. Nothing, of course, is easy. Simple? Yes, but it takes time and requires awareness, cultural acceptance, structural support, and recognition.

Tools used to help sustain 5S culture

There are many ways of helping to sustain a 5S culture, many of them using Visual Factory. These include:

- Slogans and poster campaigns
- Photos and storyboards
- Regular audits and reviews
- Newsletters incorporating success stories and 5S mission statement
- Pocket manuals
- Clear Standards
- Effective training

Why SUSTAIN?

How many times, as human beings, have we begun a project only to slowly lose momentum as our days are crowded out with the here and now? As the smoke clears, the next time we look, it turns out that we've given up! There is probably a garage somewhere where a matchstick model of St Paul's Cathedral sits languishing at the back, complete but for a missing dome. If you were to analyse the difference between success and failure, the irony is that most people who fail may have done 98% of what is required to succeed. The same danger applies to 5S. We make a tremendous effort to organise and clean our workplace; there lies the majority of the effort yet all of it will be wasted if we don't SUSTAIN it.

The benefits of sustain are that it makes 5S routine, sustains all improvements we have made and builds on these. It maintains agreed procedures and ensures that we do not fall back to our old ways.

5S SUMMARY

We have spent a lot of time discussing the elements of 5S. Let us just remind ourselves of the benefits:

- It improves safety.
- It offers a structured approach to organising the workplace.
- It is applicable to everyone from the General Manager to process operators.
- It helps improves productivity.
- It helps improves quality.
- It improves morale and teamwork.
- People actually enjoy working in a clean, organised, high quality, successful and safe environment.

The beauty of 5S is that installing it does not have to be expensive. It probably requires very little more than we already have. Improvements should be inexpensive. Ironically, the more money we spend, the less ingenuity we use to find solutions. The low cost - no cost approach should always be encouraged as a starting point.

Management is right to be suspicious when the newly fired-up 5S team appears with a shopping list of expensive options. If these are submitted straight away the management is likely to turn them down. The key to selling 5S is to implement some quick hits where benefits are clearly delivered. The management will be more likely to consider more medium to long-term costly options once they have seen success. Small incremental improvements are better than attempting a giant step-change. Don't try and change the world in one hit. It's very much like eating an elephant. Best done in bite-size chunks over a reasonably long period of time!

5S Exercise:

Perhaps you would like to visualize your workplace:
- Think of one item you could get rid of
- Think of one item you could relocate more efficiently
- Think of one item or area that would benefit from cleaning
- Think of a routine you could create to avoid the above
- Think of conditions you could create that would promote this routine

So, what's stopping you?

FACTORY LAYOUT

We have covered some elements of factory and workplace layout when we discussed set-in-order. Before we jump in with both feet and begin marking out the workplace in excruciating detail, however, consider this; it is highly likely when we get to the module covering Value Stream Mapping in Book 3 that we completely reorganise the current layout.

When working in the semiconductor plant, one of the members of the lean project team was a young, enthusiastic shift manager who, early on in the project, believed he had seen the end state. He came up with some very detailed layout drawings to support his ideas. I could not fault his enthusiasm for lean but I had to let him down gently saying his ideas were premature. Weeks later, when we had collected enough data and looked at value stream mapping the process, the solution to a radical reorganisation of the area dropped out naturally from the analysis. He came to me, grinning, with his drawings in his hand. 'Load of boll**ks aren't they?' he smiled. 'I suppose you knew it would look like this (pointing to the new layout) all along, didn't you?'

I explained that no, I didn't know what the final layout would look like when he brought his ideas to me, we had yet to do the analysis. I had ideas about the elements we might employ but certainly had not prejudged the outcome.

We will return to layout again when we get to Book 3, but in the meantime, there is one element we can introduce regardless.

Location Indicators

As part of the SET IN ORDER phase, we have seen the need to allocate a place for everything and ensure that everything is in its place. Once all superfluous materials are removed from the workspace, locations can be prepared for containers and items needed for the process. In allocating locations, it is important to

128

limit the space physically and visually. In this way, we prevent accumulation of too many containers. The containers should be sized for the standard number of parts. We will discuss deciding the optimum number of parts when we consider pull and kanbans in Book 2.

For each location, we should allocate an address for each item. This can be labelled with the location, correct name or part number and the correct quantity with maximum and minimum indicators. The information and preparation for this should be under constant review.

Location Indicators

Aspect	Method
Location indicators	Address signboards Location / limit lines Labels
Set limits	Height lines Fixed length racking Std container sizes
Danger indicators	Walkways Danger signs

We will return to layout in a later book when we discuss the use of Kanbans, but for now, it is time to summarise the steps we need to take to create stability in our organisation.

CREATING STABILITY – SUMMARY

So, here we are, at the end of the first and most important stage to becoming a truly lean enterprise. If you do no more than follow the logic of this first stage, you will already have substantial improvements in your productivity and profitability.

I appreciate there is a lot of detail in the book. If you are like me, you will retain a small proportion of what you have read. No problem, the book is always here to remind you and fill in the blanks. To help you get the most from the topics covered, I summarise the 'nuggets' of this modest book on the next page. You can use this list as a template for creating stability in your organisation.

I hope you have found the book of interest and of value. I often relate to training groups the story of the young agricultural machinery salesman trying to convince a grizzled old farmer the virtue of purchasing the latest generation of farm machinery. "It will radically improve your productivity," he concluded.

"Son," replied the farmer, "if I could farm half as well as I already know how to, I'd be doing twice as well as I am!"

It's highly likely that you were aware of a large portion of what you have read. Perhaps there are elements of it you already apply. Like the farmer, maybe you already know enough to be doing better than you are at the moment.

Please use this book, therefore, as a spur to get you started again and to focus your efforts to create the stability essential to create a truly lean enterprise. If you do this, you will not fail. Trust me, I'm an engineer!

David Syl

February 2018

- Make sure you have the right **metrics** in place
- Focus on **productivity** or standard labour hours recovered
- When confronting the challenges of your enterprise, spend time **defining the problem.** To brush over or overlook this step is to waste vital effort
- Identify the **seven wastes** in your business
- Use **the Seven Tools of Quality** to determine how to reduce them
- Do not overlook the value of **flowcharting** in this process
- Once the solution is identified, capture it as a **Standard Operating Procedure** (SOP)
- Organise the workplace using **5S**
- Remember the most important step, **Sustain**
- Use **Visual Factory** and **Visual Control** to simplify factory layout and report progress
- Introduce **Andon** and identify the **Natural Workgroup**
- Introduce **TPM**
- Work carefully with service departments to introduce **autonomous maintenance**

By the Same Author

Leadership,
A Formula for Success

Do you often think you've got the right people but not the right result?

Instead of changing people, learn to 'change' your people by changing your leadership style. In this book you will learn...

- A Formula for Leadership as profound as $E = MC^2$
- The Power of Behaviour
- How your team can become Winners and Heroes
- Leadership is as simple as A-B-C
- How to harness the Vanilla Effect and watch motivation soar
- The 5 key steps to build trust and rapport
- The Assertiveness Toolbox
- How to supercharge your team for success
- Ten proven steps to successful Leadership

The book is based on a ten week leadership training programme which reached the finals of the National Training Awards and has delivered measureable, lasting results since 1997.

David Sykes is an experienced manager and trainer. A graduate chemical engineer, he has spent the majority of his career in man-management. Throughout he has shared his knowledge and experience of building and motivating successful teams.

Training Solutions In 2005, he founded Vanilla Training Solutions Ltd, a training consultancy dedicated to helping organisations excel. Having strong inter-personal skills he has coached and mentored managers and team leaders, particularly in their early careers.

Reviews

***** Real practical advice to improve your leadership skills, delivered in an entertaining and informative manner., 17 Jun. 2016
Andrew Wilson

Let me start by saying that I had the pleasure of working alongside David a few years ago. My abiding memory of our time together was the continuous and sometimes hilarious stories that he told regarding human behaviour. All the stories were pertinent and interesting and always somehow related back to a book or a management theory. I learnt over the year that we worked together that David was an ambassador of leadership, such was his passion for the subject.

Leadership is an enormous subject and one that I find fascinating and frustratingly hard to grasp such is the breadth of knowledge and opinion on the subject. What David has achieved in this book is singularly impressive. As an author, I know how hard it is to tackle a large topic without being totally consumed by it and paralysed to a point that you do not know where to start. I have found in my own experience that only through truly knowing your subject can you navigate around it with sufficient dexterity to write a book worth reading. In Leadership - a formula for success, David has accomplished something I have not seen in any other leadership text I have read in my 25 years of management; he has managed to cover a veritable smorgasbord of theory with a light-fingered dexterity only a master of the subject can do, and he has managed to do it in an entertaining and informative way. Many of the topics in this book are, on their own, heavy reading in the source texts, but David

134

has managed to make them relevant by showing how they operate in the context of other management theories on the subject and brought them to life with real-life examples.

If you are looking for a source text on the subject of leadership, this book should form a foundation block in your reading library. You should not underestimate what you can learn from this book, it is easy to read and entertaining, and that is its secret; you will glide through the pages absorbing page on page of good sound tried and tested advice. You will learn things that you can put into practice immediately that will improve your leadership skills.

I recommend this book without hesitation.

***** Maslow meets Red Dwarf!, 12 Jun. 2016
Paul Hughes MSc FCIL

Any leadership book that combines 'real life' experiences coupled with academic analogies and Red Dwarf is a definite hit! You'll read it, make notes all over it and use it!

***** As a reader you feel like you are in the same room having a conversation ..., 23 Jun. 2016
John Aizlewood

David has captured the chemistry of people leadership in this very 'easy to read' book. It is packed with real-life examples that you can relate to and analyse. As a reader, you feel like you are in the same room having a conversation and it gets you thinking how you can deal with a similar situation, with the benefit of David's hindsight. Don't just read it, use it. Great practical tests as you go along that embed the theory set out in distinct chapters. After reading it you feel motivated to become a better leader. So, what are you waiting for? Click "add to basket" now!

***** I loved this book....27 July 2016
Amazon Customer
I loved this book and having completed it 4 weeks ago I can now see a difference in myself and how I behave at work. I like the approach the book took where at times it felt more like a conversation than a textbook and the practical examples give good context to the theory being discussed and its relevance for your daily working life. The module approach worked for me and I have been encouraging my colleagues and anyone who will listen how they need to give the book a chance and they won't be disappointed

***** What a great read....3 September 2016
Nicolas Nixon, Supply Chain Director, Coca-Cola Enterprises
What a great read. If you are a front-line manager or middle manager, this is an excellent book.   Practical examples, anecdotes and models to help your leadership style. It is a book to get you thinking. Congratulations on a fantastic piece of work.

***** It's Brilliant....27th November 2017
Jason Davenhill, Performance Coach, Inflow Performance Ltd
C.H. pointed me in the direction of your book, Leadership, a Formula for Success. I can honestly say it is the best book on management and people stuff I have read. It's brilliant.

An Engineer's Guide to Influencing and Persuading

People do business with people they know, like & trust...

Without authority over people, if we are to achieve the results demanded of us by ourselves and our organisation, we have to have POWER WITH PEOPLE. Regardless of their purpose, all business is ultimately people business and understanding people is the key to our success. Only by learning how to influence and persuade, therefore, can we get what we want. In this book you will learn:

- The Power of Behaviour
- The five key steps to building trust and rapport
- Influencing is as simple as A-B-C
- The Assertiveness Toolbox
- How to motivate people to help you
- The Lure of WIIFT (What's In It For Them?)
- How to choose the right words
- The Five-Step Plan for Influencing

If you want to know more about people, what drives them and motivates them and how you can use this knowledge to get what you want, this is the book for you.

David Sykes is an experienced manager and trainer. A graduate chemical engineer, he has spent the majority of his career in man-management. Throughout he has shared his knowledge and experience of building and motivating successful teams.

ISBN 978-1-326-82281-1

In 2005, he founded Vanilla Training Solutions Ltd, a training consultancy dedicated to helping organisations excel. Having strong inter-personal skills he has coached and mentored managers and team leaders, particularly in their early careers.

www.ingramcontent.com/pod-product-compliance
Lightning Source LLC
Chambersburg PA
CBHW071443180526
45170CB00001B/441